MW00577053

# Teaching Cultural Dexterity in Creative Writing

Research in Creative Writing

Series Editors for this edition:

Janelle Adsit (Humboldt State University, USA)
Conchitina Cruz (University of the Philippines)
James Ryan (University of Wisconsin-Madison, USA)

Showcasing the most innovative research and field-defining scholarship surrounding Creative Writing Studies, Research in Creative Writing strives to define and demonstrate the best practices for creative writing pedagogy both inside and out of the academy. It wrestles with the core issues at the heart of the field such as whether the craft can really be taught; the ethical and moral issues surrounding the practice of creative writing; and the impact of teaching established lore. Responsive to emerging exigencies in the field and open to interdisciplinary and diverse contexts for creative writing, this series is designed to advance the field and push the boundaries of Creative Writing Studies. This series benefits from the guidance of, and collaboration with, the Creative Writing Studies Organization.

Editorial board members:

Ching-In Chen (Sam Houston State University, USA)
Farid Matuk (University of Arizona, USA)

**Published titles**

*The Place and the Writer: International Intersections of Teacher Lore and Creative Writing Pedagogy,* edited by Marshall Moore and Sam Meekings
*Digital Voices: Podcasting in the Creative Writing Classroom,* Leigh Camacho Rourks and Saul Lemerond
*A-Z of Creative Writing Methods,* edited by Francesca Rendle Short, Julienne Van Loon, David Carlin, Peta Murray, Stayci Taylor and Deborah Wardle
*Craft Consciousness and Artistic Practice in Creative Writing,* Benjamin Ristow

Creative Writing Studies (CWS) is a field that exists at the interstices of creative writing, aesthetics, fine arts, composition, rhetoric, creativity studies, critical ethnic and queer studies, and literary studies and in countries around the world is regularly housed in departments and programs such as Liberal Arts, Cultural Studies, Creative Practice, Writing Studies, and Language. While there are few courses and programs that take the name "Creative Writing Studies" explicitly, the field is practiced whenever creative writing pedagogy, aesthetic theory for writers, craft-criticism, fictocriticism are studied deliberately.

*Research in Creative Writing* is a new series from Bloomsbury Academic designed to advance the academic field of Creative Writing Studies by publishing field-defining scholarly manuscripts. The series wrestles with the core issues of Creative Writing Studies: What is creative writing? What insights are currently emerging at the intersection of creative writing teaching and practice? What is the relation between the practices of creative writing and the practices of social justice? How does technology influence and inform creative writing practice? What kinds of creative writing happen inside the academy, and what sort of knowledge and ways of thinking do these practices produce? What kinds of creative writing happen outside the academy, and what meaning do these practices have for their participants?

Books in this series will explore all of these questions and more in an effort to build the research conversation that accompanies creative production.

# Teaching Cultural Dexterity in Creative Writing

Micah McCrary

BLOOMSBURY ACADEMIC
LONDON • NEW YORK • OXFORD • NEW DELHI • SYDNEY

BLOOMSBURY ACADEMIC
Bloomsbury Publishing Plc
50 Bedford Square, London, WC1B 3DP, UK
1385 Broadway, New York, NY 10018, USA
29 Earlsfort Terrace, Dublin 2, Ireland

BLOOMSBURY, BLOOMSBURY ACADEMIC and the Diana logo are
trademarks of Bloomsbury Publishing Plc

First published in Great Britain 2023

Series design by Eleanor Rose
Cover image © Trompinex/iStock

A catalogue record for this book is available from the British Library.

A catalog record for this book is available from the Library of Congress.

ISBN: HB: 978-1-3502-3713-1
ePDF: 978-1-3502-3714-8
eBook: 978-1-3502-3715-5

Series: Research in Creative Writing

Typeset by Deanta Global Publishing Services, Chennai, India

To find out more about our authors and books visit www.bloomsbury.com and
sign up for our newsletters.

*To my students, for their efforts.*
*To my teachers, for their care.*
*And to David, forever loved and missed.*

# Contents

# Tables

# Acknowledgments

My most immediate thanks extend to Lucy Brown, whose most incredible patience has guided me to complete this book through so many unforeseen circumstances. I'm grateful to you in a greater capacity than I can express.

I send additional gratitude to Janelle Adsit, Conchitina Cruz, James Ryan, and Aanchal Vij, through whom my thinking and conversations about these chapters' subjects have developed—and without whom this project would not have been possible. To Janelle, especially: I so value your insightful curiosity, and your kindness even within uncertainty.

Many thanks additionally extend to various colleagues, community members, and loved ones around the globe, all of whom have helped me see this through: Christine Adams, Indie Anderson, Aaron Babcock, Zoë Bossiere, Yavanna Brownlee, Gabriela Castañeda-Jimenez, Sylvia Chan, Ana Cortés Lagos, Kristin Distel, Sherrie Gradin, Kate Hanzalik, Allie Hoback, Mara Holt, Theodore Hutchinson, Wes Jamison, Sinae Lee, Eric LeMay, Kelly Masterson, Jeffrey McCambridge, Judith and Robert McCrary, Sarah Minor, Ona Narbutas, S. D. C. Parker, Emily Pifer, Inès Pujos, Derek Robbins, and Tatiana Uhoch. I thank you for the energy and time dedicated to any discussion and/or reading through the ideas in this project—your help is far from undervalued.

I'm finally grateful to Alden Library, American Village, Amtrak, Bird Library, Château d'Aine (Azé), Château de Joudes Saint Amour, Domaine d'Aurabelle, Donkey Coffee & Espresso, La Mazure, the McCrary family home, Recess Coffee House & Roastery, and Stout Beard Brewing Co. Without your support, I would have had neither the energy nor the space to complete the work required for this project.

# Beyond Belonging

## An Introduction

In June 2020, I attended a Black Lives Matter rally in the downtown area of present-day Syracuse, New York, following George Floyd's murder and the protests that amassed in response not just to the instance of police brutality that took Floyd's life—but also in response to the more widespread instances of police brutality afflicting racially minoritized (though mostly Black) people throughout North America in the twenty-first century. Since we'd also been amid a global health emergency caused by the novel Covid-19 virus, by the time of the rally I'd already been processing issues of inequity relevant to minoritized and marginalized (e.g., racially visible, nonnative English, disabled, queer, and low-income) communities. Especially when individuals within these communities have been student-authors in my own courses and when I, myself, fit within them as a nonwhite queer person, I'd also thought about how minoritized/marginalized student-authors have worked through their own perceptions of (in)equity through their writing in my classrooms— especially when this inequity has been the result of racialized, gendered, religious, and homophobic (and other) violence.[1]

Back to the rally: There was a queer Black woman who gave a speech, and something she said resonated with me not just in terms of my general thinking about inequity but also in regard to my own place in creative writing (CW) education given my identity: The woman said, without a single pause in her breath: "If the revolution ain't intersectional, then it ain't a revolution." This led to the crowd's claps and cheers, toward a shared understanding that the hashtag many were familiar with shouldn't have been #BlackLivesMatter but #AllBlackLivesMatter—centering queer Black lives, incarcerated Black lives, disabled Black lives, and so many more. And since this very notion also became confirmed that summer by Black Unitarian Universalists/BLUUs (a faith community I'd joined months prior) the emphasis of the hashtag hit home for me even more.[2]

This book project has, then, from the word *go*, set out to "reform" CW in higher education spaces both throughout North America (where I'm based) and in transnational contexts. But also, in processing what the rally speaker had said and applying it to all that I'd already considered about CW and my place within it, I'd been brought to ask some of my own questions, like: *What might CW's "revolution" look like?* And, *if revolutions must be intersectional, then what would an* intersectional revolution *mean for creative writing?* Finally, especially in the context of nonfiction (which I study, practice, and teach) and within which student-authors in my own courses have processed some of their most difficult thoughts and experiences, *how might an intersectional CW revolution remain adaptive to student-authors' culturally specific identities?*

## Calls for Change

I eventually began thinking through questions like these through the lens of monthly virtual BLUU meetings (which routinely emphasized foundational principles rooted in Unitarian Universalism) and as a result began imagining that, when adapted to pedagogy, these might also take the form of a set of "principles of pedagogical practice." These could strive toward:[3]

1. The inherent worth and dignity of every student.
2. Justice, equity, and compassion in student-teacher relations.
3. Acceptance of one another and encouragement toward educational growth in our class communities.
4. A free and responsible search for truth, meaning, and knowledge.
5. The right of conscience and the use of democracy within our class communities as well as with how classroom knowledge extends into societies.
6. The goal of equity, accessibility, and inclusion for all within diverse class communities.
7. Respect for the interdependent web of knowledge, to which all students and educators belong.
8. A journey toward educational wholeness by way of diverse, transcultural, and compassionate class communities, which dismantle forms of

supremacy and oppression, including, but not limited to: systemic racism, nationalism, and patriarchy.

I've imagined this toward working through many of the considerations present in David Mura's *A Stranger's Journey: Race, Identity, and Narrative Craft in Writing* (2018) as a foundational text for one of my courses (detailed further in the Appendices). Mura helps to position (creative) writing as a "call to change"—notably, that as authors "[w]e start to write a book in order to become the person who finishes the book."[4] Mura perhaps clinches this by encouraging student-authors to further consider their writing as a process of self-change, asking: "What are the ways you need to change yourself—or your life—in order to finish the book you are writing?"[5]

I immediately connected this to Jenny Boully, who writes in *The Body: An Essay* (2007) that "[e]verything I do, I do because I know I am dying" and that "[a]s we get old, we have more to think about in less time—we must think of more in a compressed amount of time."[6] Time has certainly felt compressed for me throughout the Covid-19 pandemic, and as I continue thinking about ways *I've* needed to change myself/my life in order to finish this book, the strongest conclusions I've arrived at are that my personal "revolution" must remain just as intersectional as contemporary calls for change around antiracism—or the fact that this book chooses to center creative writing. In essence, this book project is one I've needed to pursue by embracing my whole self as a queer, multiracial (of Black, First American, and European descent) cisgender man of US nationality with plurilingual ambitions and a habit of religious study.[7] I've needed to pursue the book by embracing wholeheartedly the intersections of my identity, considering how best to use my positioning to affect helpful change within writing class communities.

## Parallel Practice(s)

Throughout this book I've considered issues of equity, inclusion, diversity, and internationalization in CW curricula, which have led me to develop and teach courses in literary/creative nonfiction that use as their foundation Janelle Adsit's "threshold concepts in creative writing." In Adsit's paper "The Writer and Meta-Knowledge about Writing: Threshold Concepts in Creative Writing" (more fully developed in Adsit's book *Toward an Inclusive Creative Writing: Threshold Concepts to Guide the Literary Curriculum*, 2017), these threshold concepts are wonderfully tailored toward curricula for student-authors in fiction and even poetry; the circumstances for student-authors in nonfiction, however, require different considerations (and, I've observed, are also less commonly discussed in creative writing studies). For this reason, throughout this book I strongly propose combining Adsit's concepts with a framework of cultural dexterity.

To clarify further, *cultural dexterity* itself emerged from a 2019 PACTS (The Provider Awareness and Cultural Dexterity Toolkit for Surgeons) study, which I initially came across during my doctoral study while teaching composition to nurses matriculating from their RN to BSN degrees, wherein my courses (usually centering illness narratives and graphic medicine) contributed to student-authors' perspectives on patient education and, about which, these nurses routinely explored ways of incorporating our course materials into their own workplaces.

The PACTS study, as I've learned about it through teaching, has intended to "test the impact of a new curriculum [. . .] on surgical residents' cross-cultural knowledge, attitudes, and skills surrounding the care of patients from diverse cultural backgrounds, as well as clinical and patient-reported health outcomes for patients treated by surgical residents undergoing this training."[8] In a pivotal parallel to this book, PACTS' cultural dexterity curriculum is also "comprised of four educational modules on [1] establishing trust in the physician-patient relationship, [2] communicating effectively with patients with limited English proficiency, [3] discussing informed consent, and [4] issues surrounding pain management."[9] On top of broadening the goals initially set out by cultural competence/y models, I'm drawn toward a cultural dexterity framework by way of the four modules within the PACTS curriculum. And, though this book doesn't center medicine, it nonetheless centers the nonfiction student-author in similar ways to how cultural dexterity in medical education attempts to center the patient.

In effect, PACTS employs cultural dexterity to reach beyond notions of cultural competence/y, offering a working definition for *cultural dexterity* as referring to "a set of skills and cognitive practices used to maximize communication across multiple dimensions of cultural diversity and deviates from the concept of cultural competency in that it does not demand that learners associate certain practices and behaviors with individuals based on generalizations."[10] This can also apply to a CW context for graduate student instructors (GSIs) and their own student-authors, pointing toward how cultural competence/y may carry too much potential for such a model to allow for instances of essentializing (i.e., "associating certain practices and behaviors with individuals based on generalizations") while students read the culturally diverse work of professional literary authors as well as their peers.

The outcomes expressed in the cultural dexterity curriculum, if integrated within CW pedagogies, can increase CW educators' (including GSIs) attention toward inclusion and diversity in their classrooms. For example, paralleling cultural dexterity "Module 1" with CW can foster more careful considerations around power, trust, and authority within the relationship between the nonfiction student-author and the CW educator, as well as between student-authors as class community members. Paralleling "Module 2" can then posture GSIs toward an expansion of CW's pedagogical practices reaching beyond the hegemony of English monolingualism. A careful parallel of "Module 3" can offer more common discussions of affect and ethics in CW—specifically in the nonfiction workshop space, where student-authors often share writing about their own lives. This finally includes a potential parallel for "Module 4," wherein the contexts around what's admitted or confessed in the classroom about student-authors' lives might be centered around actual experiences of discrimination, oppression, trauma, abuse, and other forms of social violence—and which CW educators (especially as GSIs) aren't always directly told to prepare for when learning to teach nonfiction. I therefore see these parallels as a usable framing for nonfiction/CW pedagogies, and to make this clear throughout my chapters, I pivot the modules' implications toward an exigence for a CW (nonfiction) context.

## Overview

Especially given that the workshop model has been the "default" mode of CW instruction for decades, the first chapter, "Difficult Dialogues: Toward a Trauma-Informed Creative Writing Workshop," explores ways to prepare GSIs for nonnormative workshop models attuned to student-authors who choose to compose nonfiction centered on traumatic experience. It especially considers how the traditional North American CW workshop (aka the "Iowa Model") might perpetuate aspects of trauma within the model's very execution, making it a potentially complicated pedagogy for undergraduate student-authors writing about lived experiences of race-based traumatic stress (RBTS) or sexual trauma. The chapter endorses a shift away from normative workshop pedagogies, alongside an insistence upon an openness toward difficult discussions in the class community/workshop. In particular, the chapter imagines ways to generate praxis for GSIs, regarding how lived experiences, resilience, and cultural frames of reference brought into the class community might be aided by a trauma-informed (TI) framework as applied to the nonfiction workshop.

The second chapter, "Writing Lives at the Roundtable: Toward Teaching Students-as-Authors," emphasizes the cultural dexterity framework as employed toward "establishing trust" among the student-author, the GSI, and the wider CW class community, by way of showing students how to recognize themselves *as* authors. It not only focuses on ways GSIs might practice creating classroom environments within which trust can be built but also considers the varied reasons why student-authors with minoritized/marginalized identities might enter the classroom harboring distrust of power structures in the first place. Considering a transnational potential for cultural dexterity here, the chapter then aims to re-center student-author agency on top of an increased focus on effective peer communication between student-authors from differing backgrounds.

"Why Bother in English? On Creative Writing's Translingual Potential" more explicitly outlines how cultural dexterity in CW attempts to focus on student-authors from various language backgrounds—especially in the goal to examine how, for instance, the disciplines of writing studies and English Language Teaching (ELT) have long battled English-only policies. It's now CW's turn. This works toward ways translingual models for nonfiction classrooms might nudge GSIs closer to recognizing and incorporating language diversity, rather than treating the CW classroom space as only monolingual (English), and additionally highlights the increased number of international and nonnative English student-authors in my own courses throughout recent years.

Because "Before and Beyond Genre: Critically Considering Craft in the Nonfiction Classroom" confronts the institutional realities of CW programs, the chapter uses cultural dexterity to discuss CW education as well as the expectations around such an education for nonfiction student-authors. It contrasts the expectation(s) of higher education institutions with those CW communities outside the "ivory tower," in effort to get GSIs (and their own student-authors) to better reflect on and critique the reasons behind their learning to practice CW specifically within college/university environments. This can be helpful for any GSIs bridging gaps between undergraduate student-authors in their courses and themselves, all of whom study/practice nonfiction in a higher education context.

"Beyond Genesis: A Transcultural Exigency for Research in Creative Writing" further discusses how emphases on research in CW (nonfiction) can move curricula toward more common instances of "cross-cultural knowledge." It discusses how research in CW isn't just an important practice for nonfiction student-authors but stretches further to explore *how* research based on a cultural dexterity framework can help reach the outcomes set out by CW curricula that intend for such research to refine student-authors' communication skills—specifically within milieus that prioritize inclusion and diversity.

A combination of the final two chapters, "Toward Critical Concepts in the Creative Writing Classroom: Some Reflections on Course Designs" and "Where We've Been, Where We're Going: Considerations and Continuations," helps GSIs consider what it might mean for there to be an "Honor Roll of Graduate Creative Writing Programs" (à la Stephanie Vanderslice) in the context of curricular design centering inclusion and diversity. This is specifically done through a lens of how such programs might work toward the potential to reform CW education using a cultural dexterity framework. It therefore "brings the book home" by reminding GSIs that, while there are institutional parameters around how CW programs are structured, there's still a grand potential for reevaluating CW education toward the goal of centering the student-author—rather than centering either genre or "craft." This invites faculty and GSIs together to consider their own positions in CW education and allows both parties to simultaneously consider methodologies and locales—that is, the *why* those of us involved in CW do what we do, as well as the *where* we've chosen to do it.

Finally, it's crucial that CW educators can look toward broader notions of inclusion and diversity by way of cultural dexterity in CW, especially following the leads of authors, editors, and researchers like Janelle Adsit, Felicia Rose

Chavez, Sherry Quan Lee, David Mura, Matthew Salesses, and more, who all pose necessary questions for educators around ways to encounter a diversity of texts/authors in CW classrooms for the benefit of diverse student-authors. Pedagogical joy can be found not just in reform (or revision?) that creates room for voices not found on syllabi as often as they otherwise could be, but this can also be achieved by avoiding the privileging of *craft*—centering, instead, the culturally situated identities of literary authors.

## Casting a Wide(r) Net

A final context for this book lies with the growing number of GSIs assigned to teach (particularly introductory) nonfiction courses, in combination with the growing number of those in graduate CW programs in general. The book therefore works to help prepare nonfiction GSIs to hold discussions with the diversity of their own student-authors about complex aspects of lived experience as they tend to appear in classroom texts—ideally not only then better preparing them to teach nonfiction themselves but also moving toward a greater consideration of how they hone their writing practices as nonfiction authors.

As someone who was once a graduate student in nonfiction programs myself and, additionally, as a nonwhite and queer author, there are conversations I wish I could have had as a student among other minoritized/marginalized student-authors and faculty. These are conversations I now wish to generate for those engaging in twenty-first-century CW education. This is also tiered, in that it attempts to connect the seasoned CW educator, the GSI learning to teach creative writing, and graduate and undergraduate nonfiction student-authors—altogether offering the discussions relevant and necessary for a contemporary landscape in CW/nonfiction in higher education.

This is of course not limited to the United States. Especially toward addressing the growing number of international student-authors in CW courses, as well as being able to converse with student-authors about the traditions they themselves bring into classrooms, the book casts a wide net—allowing those participating in CW education to consider its interventions beyond just one's geography, ethnicity, nationality, or choice of genre practice.

The book's aim finally focuses on the numerous student-authors choosing to practice CW in higher education communities. It therefore highlights the issues inherent in these choices—some of which have been imposed upon those who are "certain" that they need a BA/BFA/M(F)A/PhD in creative writing in order to "achieve" authorship, for example.[11] Perhaps most importantly, however, this book allows for conversations taking place that can precede the genre- and craft-related expectations so often already set before student-authors, and extends considerations around a student-centered CW pedagogy to remain an inclusive and attentive practice.

# Notes

1 I use *nonwhite* to establish a deliberate binary here. Colloquially, at least at the time of this writing, we don't use vocabulary like "Black supremacy," "Native supremacy," "Asian supremacy," "Latine supremacy," etc. The term is always "white supremacy," and for this reason I'll often refer to the racially minoritized/ marginalized people within this binary as *nonwhite*.

2 Like many for whom the pandemic affected their religious considerations, on top of BLUU I also joined the campus Buddhist chaplaincy at my home institution.

3 Adapted from the Seven Principles of Unitarian Universalism.

4 Mura, David. *A Stranger's Journey: Race, Identity, and Narrative Craft in Writing*. The University of Georgia Press, 2018.

5 Ibid., p. 258.

6 Boully, Jenny. *The Body: An Essay*. Essay Press, 2007.

7 I'll detail later in the book that the three Native heritages I descend from are Mvskoke Creek (some of whose documentation includes the term "Native American"), Chahta (using "Indian"), and Chikasha (using "First American"). Though relatives have used both "Native American" and "Indian" when discussing family history, I've chosen throughout this book to use "Native" and "First American" depending on context.

8 Haider, Adil. "The Provider Awareness and Cultural Dexterity Toolkit for Surgeons Trial." *The Provider Awareness and Cultural Dexterity Toolkit for Surgeons Trial—Full Text View—ClinicalTrials.gov*, 2018, https://clinicaltrials.gov /ct2/show/NCT03576495#wrapper.

9 Ibid.

10 Ibid.

11 See, for example, Patrick Bizzaro's and Michael McClanahan's "Putting Wings on the Invisible: Voice, Authorship, and the Authentic Self."

# Further Reading

Bizzaro, Patrick and Michael McClanahan. "Putting Wings on the Invisible: Voice, Authorship, and the Authentic Self." *Can It Really Be Taught? Resisting Lore in Creative Writing Pedagogy*, edited by Kelly Ritter and Stephanie Vanderslice, Boynton/Cook Heinemann, 2007, pp. 77–90.

Haake, Katharine. *What Our Speech Disrupts: Feminism and Creative Writing Studies.* National Council of Teachers of English, 2000.

hooks, bell. *Teaching to Transgress: Education as the Practice of Freedom.* Routledge, 1996.

hooks, bell. *Teaching Community: A Pedagogy of Hope.* Routledge, 2003.

hooks, bell. *Teaching Critical Thinking: Practical Wisdom.* Routledge, 2009.

Leahy, Anna, editor. *Power and Identity in the Creative Writing Classroom: The Authority Project.* Multilingual Matters, 2005.

1

# Difficult Dialogues

## Toward a Trauma-Informed Creative Writing Workshop

Student-authors in North America learn about the creative writing (CW) workshop model as being integral to traditional CW pedagogies either as undergraduates or during their graduate study. They may eventually come to see the model as a CW cornerstone, and because it so often seems to have been established as the status quo (likely since the advent of the Iowa Writers' Workshop in 1936), it can feel like going along with this cornerstone/tradition is just part and parcel with CW's culture in higher education throughout North America.[1]

There hasn't always been much reason for (undergraduate) student-authors to question the model, but when then they begin to teach workshops as graduate student instructors (GSIs), they might start to witness ways the model plays out for their student-authors—especially those coming from various cultural, linguistic, racialized, gendered, sexually oriented, and other backgrounds. GSIs could come to see how these backgrounds mesh with discussions of student-authors' writing—but sometimes, they don't mesh. (Sometimes, they even clash.) Sometimes this is because a student-author's familiarity with a writing subject inhabits a realm of understanding that comes across as unfamiliar or "foreign" to their peers. Sometimes this is the result of a student-author having written material that deeply affects the emotional states of others in the class community.

GSIs can begin contending with how their student-authors bring writing that's near and dear to them into introductory nonfiction workshops, to be discussed in class with the goal of receiving feedback. Live feedback is a great and necessary and helpful and even hopeful goal but questioning this feedback should also involve investigating how student-authors' lived experiences (as well as cultural repertoires) affect the interpretation and commentary of/on their classmates' work, in addition to feedback received *from* GSIs. Especially when student-authors enter twenty-first-century CW from minoritized/marginalized identities, it's worth exploring how GSIs learning to teach CW can work to address these positions as they show up in writing.

Since Module 4 for the proposed PACTS curriculum (as laid out in the Introduction of this book) is expressed toward examining "issues around pain management," this chapter focuses on the potentially traumatic/traumatizing atmosphere of CW workshops and how acknowledging such an atmosphere might better prepare GSIs to address resilience while helping student-authors share difficult "life-writing" in spaces already fraught with vulnerability.[2] A central question might encircle how pain management and resilience integration could look in CW's context, especially as student-authors potentially bring difficult experiences to the fore within CW class communities. In other words, what does (and should) it mean to "manage the pain" of nonfiction student-authors? And how can GSIs prepare to moderate such an atmosphere as they learn to teach, keeping not just the safety of their student-authors in mind but managing their own safety, as well?

Especially when class communities comprise student-authors from minoritized/marginalized backgrounds who have a difficult time bringing these backgrounds into creative writing, there must be discussion around how trauma acknowledgment and resilience might more generally manifest within a nonnormative (more on this later) CW workshop. And there must be agreement that, especially in nonfiction, any workshop space/model must first and foremost be trauma-informed. Such a (trauma-informed) space might be guided through imagining a culturally dexterous curricular outcome like the following: *In this course, student-authors will learn to respond to the difficult experiences in classmates' writing with care and through a practice of rhetorical listening.*

## Fishes Out of Water: (Normative) Workshops as Traumatizing Spaces

I care about imagining this outcome because I hope to grow into being an instructor who can facilitate workshops student-authors want to be part of rather than the kinds they dread, or those where they anticipate that their workshop experiences will entail negative emotions. I'd rather they get excited about workshops as we anticipate them in our weekly classes. And, in terms of thinking about this through the purview of pedagogy, I come to realize that the conversation I'm trying to have here highlights the fact that in regard to CW educator training/preparation, while these were conversations I was prepared to encounter through writing studies/composition pedagogies, they were missing from my CW pedagogical training. This partially arises from a feeling of being a kind of fish out of water when entering CW workshops as an educator and from not having prepared for where to take potential discussions of written traumatic experience in a CW course trajectory.

More pointedly, CW educators must understand that it's one thing for a student-author to try writing about Traumatic Experience X or Y when *only* the educator will see the student-author's work—which often happens with writing studies assignments that don't involve peer review. But since CW is more often built *around* peer review, there's greater risk that a student-author brings work into the course that triggers a peer or that causes what we recognize as traumatization, retraumatization, and/or vicarious traumatization. A culturally dexterous outcome can prepare not just CW educators for these scenarios to potentially arise in their classes, but it can help student-authors discern what to do as members of the class community as peer reviewers.

\*  \*  \*

To start contextualizing how the workshop can sometimes perform as a traumatizing space, I often read with student-authors Beth Nguyen's *Literary Hub* essay "Unsilencing the Writing Workshop," which discusses shifting away from a workshop method that's completely "silenced"—that is, following the traditional/normative "Iowa model" of ensuring the student-author scheduled for workshop remains silent while they receive an oscillation of praise and critique from classmates before getting to speak at the end of the workshop session. It's helpful to discuss with student-authors how Nguyen details changing strategies away from conducting normative workshops and toward those the student-author whose work is being discussed literally gets to speak, whereby they become encouraged to receive and address questions around their work's greater context.

Nguyen notes how this strategic change could have helped them during their own days as an MFA student. As they write:

> [w]hen I asked a group of writers how they would describe their workshop experiences, responses included: crushing, nightmare, hazing ritual, test of endurance, awful, ugh. I've heard of students drinking before their workshops; I've heard of students crying in class and after it; I've heard of students never looking at their workshopped pieces again. The word brutal is often used, as if honesty must necessarily be brutal. All of this seems to be viewed as inevitable, just part of the workshop experience, because it's balanced by the positive: detailed critiques, solid suggestions, real ideas for revision, and validation from peers and professors.[3]

I relate somewhat to Nguyen's experience in that as MFA students (and even as PhD students) it was common for us to go straight from workshop into a bar, even on those afternoons and nights when the weather would batter our bodies. Or maybe we'd try psyching ourselves up for a workshop session by taking the pressure off beforehand (also in a bar) as a clear indication that the workshop wasn't necessarily something we all *looked forward* to.

This is telling about what the workshop dynamic/atmosphere implies: that workshops are filled with tension, and that they could be happier spaces, period. Nguyen writes about this in terms of how when they began teaching nonfiction, they started perceiving the workshop space as "more delicate," noting that "when you talk about a 'text' that is true, and the author is in the room, then you are also talking about the author. No way around it. For underrepresented students especially, this can quickly become a tense, stressful environment."[4] The shift Nguyen makes here as the educator toward discussing workshop experience communicates what a revised workshop environment might entail, with Nguyen concluding that "[w]hen the writer gets to talk about what they're trying to do, they discover something more about what they actually are doing. Almost always, they reveal information that they'd been holding back. In other words, their talking within workshop, rather than at the end of it, helped them process their own process."[5]

Nguyen's classroom solution speaks to the benefits of shifting power dynamics from workshops categorized as "silenced" toward those that can be "unsilenced," especially when the workshop is inherently inclusive of the student-author's voice—becoming something more akin to a conversation instead of a debate. This way, the workshop isn't merely a volley of words between student-peers-as-critics who discuss what's "working" and what's "not working," but it's instead an atmosphere where student-authors receive answers to questions they might genuinely have as readers. Toward these ends, educators can ensure they address the traumatic implications of the normative workshop by getting rid of the "gag rule" entirely.

In a similar vein, discussing "How Can We Make the MFA More Hospitable to Writers of Color?" as a conversation between Sabina Murray and Ocean Vuong (then both MFA faculty members at the University of Massachusetts, Amherst), the class community can also learn about workshops that operate warmly rather than with frigidity. This offers suggestions for how workshops can stay receptive to nonwhite student-authors who bring their identities to the fore within their work, and the class community can note from Ocean Vuong that

> [w]hen we observe the workshop as merely a place where things must be fixed, we begin at a prescriptive stance—which can be quite detrimental to POC writers. These writers often enter the page with lexicons, vernaculars, syntax, and/or styles unfamiliar to a white patriarchal tradition, and in this prescriptive gaze, their work is often mis-read, perhaps being labeled as "wrong" or "weak" or worse, "incomprehensible."[6]

This can be a call to both white workshop student-authors and white educators, pointing to the potentially detrimental effects of the workshop when it presents as *prescriptive* toward nonwhite student-authors. This prescription doesn't aid nonwhite student-authors' learning if their white counterparts desire something else from the work so that they aren't "alienated" as readers. White workshop members' lack of familiarity with a nonwhite student-author's (culturally situated) writing subject elicits potential tension points in class, which can result in feedback that's neither helpful nor necessarily kind to the nonwhite student-author trying to work through specific aspects of their text.

Being biracial and Filipino, from the same conversation Sabina Murray notes how

> [n]ot only do I come from a misunderstood culture, I often have to fight to be recognized within this defining structure. This has made me sensitive to the various undercurrents that happen in a workshop, where emotions run high. So when you speak of surviving into a space, and that space being the workshop, that resonates with me.[7]

Both the ideas of "misunderstood culture" and "surviving into a space" are aspects of the workshop that need to be more concretely recognized. The idea of "surviving into a space," especially, should never be attributed to workshop: workshop shouldn't be somewhere one must steel themself for potential critiques/feedback that are the result of "misunderstood culture," and CW educators instead need to create ways of making the space more inviting for nonwhite participants, helping them become excited to share the cultural nuances that are or may not be immediately familiar to their white counterparts.

Facilitating the workshop space as "a site for both error and illumination at once" (Vuong) as well as one that gives "permission to discuss issues of race" (Vuong) implies that the workshop itself can serve as a space for racial discourse, leading to a stronger argument for linking race and craft—rather than the idea that craft should be "colorblind" so that workshop participants are ready to hold conversations about their peers' work while also being able to articulate their own authorial goals without shyness. In other words, because we so often write our identities into our (nonfiction) texts, our racialized positions as authors become inextricable from the writing itself.

## GSI Resources

It may be simple enough to think that as educators our primary job is working with knowledge, but it's not. The job is to work with people. And in this endeavor to work with the people (i.e., student-authors) in our classrooms, it's important to remain attentive to aspects of affect (i.e., the mood being measured by behavior) in the class community, rather than just the context/ depth of the material to be read/critiqued. And given the onus on CW educators to engineer the workshop classroom space as a trauma-informed one, especially in the context of the concerns just discussed, it's crucial for GSIs to envision how trauma-informed educational practice (TIEP) can shape the classroom space itself—more particularly, in this case, for the nonfiction workshop where student-authors may submit work focused on their own experiences of trauma.

To begin GSIs' thinking about trauma-informed educational practice, one resource could include Janice Carello's and Lisa D. Butler's article, "Practicing

What We Teach: Trauma-Informed Educational Practice," wherein Carello and Butler express an aim "to make a beginning case for applying the essential elements of TIC [trauma-informed care] to education and outline our initial efforts to develop guidelines for what we call trauma-informed educational practice (TIEP)."[8] Here, Carello and Butler offer guidelines for how educators in different spheres of higher education might enact TIEP to discern, first, how to "do no harm" in classrooms. Second, the authors aim to assess how to reduce harm overall through praxis that can avoid traumatization, retraumatization, and/or (as Carello and Butler term it) vicarious traumatization.

"To be *trauma-informed*," Carello and Butler argue

in any context, is to understand the ways in which violence, victimization, and other traumatic experiences may have impacted the lives of the individuals involved and to apply that understanding to the design of systems and provision of services so they accommodate trauma survivors' needs and are constant with healing and recovery.[9]

This could be helpful in a nonfiction course where class community members may be unaware of one another's backgrounds prior to beginning the term. Especially in scenarios where trauma can potentially be introduced/addressed by way of student-authors' writing, as Carello states in her own experience:

[i]t is not uncommon for students to write about their trauma histories in writing courses. A staple in many 1st-year composition courses (and many undergraduate creative writing seminars) is the personal essay. Journals are also common expectations, as are assignments based on books and films about individual and cultural trauma such as rape, the events of 9/11, and genocide. Even when personal writing is not assigned, students often choose to research and write about topics related to their personal trauma (Carello & Butler, 2014). In addition, because of typically small class sizes and formats, writing instructors often interact more with students than do instructors of other classes, and this type of involvement also may enable self-disclosure, both in and out of the classroom.[10]

Carello's and Butler's mention of 9/11 recalls the dozens of student-authors I've seen choose to write about their pandemic experiences. I have about eighty student-authors a semester and I'm comfortable saying that perhaps half have chosen to use their writing projects to process the information and contexts around Covid-19. Similar to what Carello and Butler report seeing, these student-authors seem to locate ways of working through trauma histories, albeit in a different and more contemporary context.

Although Carello mentions first-year composition (FYC), in the previous quotation, the additional coverage of CW courses offers an opportunity for GSIs to consider how "self-disclosure" can risk (re)traumatizing survivors in the class, whether this is other student-authors or GSIs themselves. Given that these courses are designed and conducted without a fully transparent knowledge of the life histories of others in the class community, a culturally dexterous trauma-informed (TI) framework can help accommodate student-authors and/or the GSIs in nonfiction workshops that discuss difficult experiences.

Carello and Butler crucially note that there are "five principles" that are "fundamental to creating and sustaining TI settings," these being "ensuring safety, establishing trustworthiness, maximizing choice, maximizing collaboration, and prioritizing empowerment."[11] All five could be applied directly to a culturally dexterous TI framework for CW courses. Ensuring safety, for instance, might encompass establishing transparent parameters for how class is conducted in addition to assignment outcomes—giving student-authors a measure of predictability by allowing them to know major assignments/ projects will focus on the relevant dimensions of class content. Toward establishing trustworthiness, there's also a component of transparency and vulnerability—which might look like building communication channels via the "Announcements" page on Blackboard (or another learning management system an institution utilizes), for example.

Maximizing choice could entail allowing student-authors multiple ways to access course concepts (if not the material itself) which, in CW contexts, are often readings. Exploring mixed modalities as alternatives might help to address *choice*, for example, content or topics connected to modes aside from alphanumeric text and altogether offering student-authors the option of accessing one mode over another.[12]

Maximizing collaboration might mean establishing senses of student authorship (i.e., agency) in the class community. This could accommodate not only what student-authors compose but also the course material itself—asking student-authors what they're confused about with course material and using questions around this confusion to guide class discussions. This can mean asking student-authors what about the reading *they* believe should be covered during class. To maintain transparency, the GSI could list on the projector/whiteboard what student-authors hope to discuss.

Finally, prioritizing empowerment must involve directing student-authors to explore what interests them via at least one component of the course—allowing them to compose the writing they wish to, rather than communicating rigidity around writing subjects throughout the course term. This could involve student-authors exploring different genres/subgenres/modes for what they compose in class, further offering an option of proposing their own alternative projects/assignments rather than just what's laid out in a syllabus.

Frankly, these five TI principles aren't compatible with the North American normative CW workshop model. And part of what makes this even more tricky is that when enacting TI principles in the workshop classroom, North America's normative model doesn't aim to avoid student-author (re)traumatization.

Another element is that the CW course doesn't need to be a space where all difficult writing subjects are avoided just to avoid tough conversations. In this, I especially advocate for a TI space over a "trauma-specific" approach where the objective is to address trauma head-on. Unless the GSI has had prior training in counseling/therapy, I contend that the CW space isn't one wherein a "trauma-specific" model should necessarily be implemented—the TI perspective remains the better option.[13]

\* \* \*

Before covering normative options for the workshop, there should be discussion of what workshop "normativity" (at least in North America) is in the first place, as well as how this normativity can affect the considerations of/encounters with trauma in the nonfiction course. For my part, I first discovered the normative model as a two-year college student in a course requiring periodic distribution of my work to the rest of the class community and listening to peers and the instructor provide commentary while I silently took notes. I did have a few less normative undergraduate CW experiences but being introduced to the normative model at nineteen years old made it so that I built an initial expectation that this was how all CW pedagogies would operate throughout much of my school career. An instructor could prove me wrong depending on who they were, but for the most part this was what I came to see as being CW's default mode of instruction. This was also confirmed during my MFA and PhD, where the normative workshop was further perpetuated. Normalizing this model made it so that I never needed to question it, its history, or its utility in the classroom—which wasn't something I needed to do until, as a graduate student, I became tasked with imagining how the workshops I'd teach might run.

What I attempt tackling here requires contending with some of those resistances to the normative CW workshop model. I try believing in what the workshop can do for student-authors' thinking and development, but I do so here particularly in the context of the TI workshop as a diverse class community—that is, I think through ways workshopping might help student-authors remain open to the difficulties already inherent in examining their texts. I try to believe in workshopping as neither inherently evil nor oppressive but, rather, as an opportunity for student-authors to practice engaging one another within potentially difficult dialogic situations.

Even this can be specified toward more awareness of workshop participants' and CW educators' experiences as they translate to practices of textual discussion. In this vein, GSIs might gravitate toward a resource like Vicki Lindner's essay "The Tale of Two Bethanies: Trauma in the Creative Writing Class," where Lindner discusses the potentially therapeutic outcomes/effects of their trauma-centered CW courses. Lindner details the experiences of working with two student-authors, "Bethany One" (a Women and Writing student) and "Bethany Two" (an Autobiographical Writing student). Bethany One began missing class and skipping readings, eventually revealed to Lindner to be the result of these readings (as well as class discussions) forcing her to recall a campus rape by a fraternity member during her first year.[14] Bethany Two's mother had committed suicide, purposely leaving a trail for Bethany to find her mother's body.

Lindner notes that student-authors often compose narrative nonfiction "about addiction, surviving homophobia, divorce, illness, death, and eating disorders. But the most poignant narratives—those that challenge me most as a teacher—are by victims of trauma: physical abuse and sexual abuse, incest, violent crime, war and suicide."[15] (Lindner also carefully notes how much potential exists for vicarious traumatization on their own part as these courses' instructor, when student-authors write about their difficult experiences.) In particular, we're given a description of Bethany One as a student-author, while she discussed her experience with Lindner:

juicy tears coursed down her cheeks, cutting trails through her pasty mask of make-up. I said, "No wonder you're sick—walking around with this burden of pain." In his essay, "Bearing Witness or the Vicissitudes of Listening," Dori Laub warns, "The listener to trauma comes to be a participant and a co-owner of the traumatic event: through his very listening, he comes to partially experience trauma in himself." As Bethany One's tears dissolved the rust encrusting my Egyptian trauma, I, too, started to bawl. I told her that I had also been a victim of violence. She hadn't seen a therapist, and sniffling into a Kleenex, I encouraged her to contact one.[16]

This incident offers clear enough examples of what are recognized as *vicarious traumatization* and *retraumatization*, showing how these took effect within Lindner's own experience. Lindner's crying as a response to Bethany One's experiences as written about in her narrative also compelled them perhaps not to disclose full details of what happened in Egypt (mentioned earlier in Lindner's essay) but still grazed the surface of notions that the two shared some frame of traumatic experience, over which they could now connect as instructor and student-author.

Lindner details how drawing a line in the sand between themselves and their student-author creates boundaries around authority and power—a boundary not just allowing student-authors like Bethany One to work through the narratives composed in class but also adding some measurement of protection from vicarious traumatization/retraumatization on Lindner's part. This is expressed as a measure of "discomfort at sobbing in my place of business," and how maintaining what Lindner at another point in the essay calls a "professorial identity" perhaps did much work to not just employ a boundary between Lindner and their student-authors, but also toward encouraging student-authors to do the work they'd been tasked with doing in the first place.[17]

Considering how a class community like Lindner's possibly acts as trauma-informed, Lindner concludes there were incidences when they'd overstepped as an educator—incidences wherein they thought they may have "pushed" student-authors to do too much, say too much, and write too much regarding traumatic experiences. Lindner reveals that this happened in the case of Bethany Two since, during the process of composing her work, Bethany revisited the site of her mother's suicide—which then led to her seeking immediate therapeutic treatment and medication. Lindner then backed off while recognizing this instance of retraumatization, and perhaps as a result they now remain sensitive to signals that a student is troubled: missed classes, poor work habits, anxiety combined with careless, dull writing, suicidal imagery. I invite those students in for conferences. If a student confides a personal trauma, I assume she feels ready to write about it. I credit the power of the story, but I don't gush with sympathy. I listen carefully, ask questions, and, at the same time, offer craft-based suggestions. (I steer an uncomfortable student toward corners of the traumatic experience: What happened afterwards? How did it affect your brother?) If the story is painful, I try to hear it the way a wine taster tastes wine—swish it around in my brain to get the flavour without swallowing. Still, like a Red Cross worker, prepared to duck gunshots to bring food to injured civilians, I acknowledge that my own discomfort is a necessary risk. I mitigate the peril, for myself and the student, by maintaining my professorial identity.[18]

Lindner remains explicit about their pedagogy being one that avoids vicarious traumatization and/or retraumatization, and they maintain a clear recognition of what they can "handle" in class as well as what they can't (or shouldn't attempt to). This can clue educators in to further recognizing the workshop as a potentially traumatizing space, and whether observing those like Nguyen, Murray and Vuong, or Lindner, we're guided here in a direction toward acknowledging that the workshop doesn't and shouldn't operate like other more "traditional" classrooms. The workshop isn't a large lecture hall that relies on one-way communication; it's also not a literature seminar where students mainly discuss the work of some highly esteemed author.

For nonfiction, workshop is often sharply focused on the real experiences of student-authors and how they try processing these experiences—making sense of the worlds and societies they inhabit. There must then be more specific attention to the ways this processing can play out in class communities, how to prepare student-authors to have such conversations in class, and how GSIs can prepare for conversations with student-authors as they begin to develop and practice their pedagogies.

In addition to Lindner's work, another resource comes from Rosalie Morales Kearns's essay "Voice of Authority: Theorizing Creative Writing Pedagogy," wherein Morales Kearns pointedly names the "traditional" model the *normative workshop*—in this case, the workshop becomes something akin to a culture for student-authors in institutions of North American higher education to enter when they've decided to pursue CW. This is what I ultimately rail against—though numerous others have all but abandoned the efficacy of the workshop, I express straightforwardly that it isn't the workshop in general that I'm hesitant about, but, rather, just its normative model.

According to Morales Kearns, a workshop meets criteria for *normativity* when:

(1) The author is prohibited from speaking during discussion of her or his work (the "gag rule"); (2) discussion focuses (sometimes exclusively) on purported "flaws" in the work; and (3) while the existence of a "flaw" implies that the author is deviating from some norm, participants do not articulate what norms they have in mind when they detect "flaws." This conventional format has no name, and its very namelessness, I think, hinders us from truly understanding it and imagining alternatives.[19]

I've laid out #1 above regarding the "gag rule." For #2, with discussion focused on "purported flaws in the work," this came to feel normal throughout many of my undergraduate and graduate experiences, in that instructors often asked for a combination of peer critique and praise for the student-author scheduled for workshop. Sometimes this began a discussion around a workshopped text using the question "So, what's not working?" before pursuing the question "So, what *is* working?"

While my experiences haven't always lined up with these points (in that I don't remember bringing work into class that was so culturally nuanced that I'd worry other workshop participants might reject my content), I do understand the experience of discussing "flaws" in my work as parallel to what should be praised in the work. As a student-author I had to learn whose feedback I valued/respected most in the course aside from the instructor and discern how to posture any feedback toward potential revision, so that a next iteration of my draft could be given an instructor's stamp of approval and I could receive my well-earned grade.

I don't imagine it's so difficult to practice alternatives to the normative workshop as Morales Kearns describes it. And, it might even be more pressing to involve ways criteria for workshop normativity have been established in CW while also offering a view of the workshop as a kind of social artifact/ construction.[20]

"When I started my MFA," as Morales Kearns writes,

[a]nd first encountered the gag rule, it struck me as a distinctly raced practice—specifically, a Euro-American practice. The expectations about

spoken interaction that I have internalized as a woman of Puerto Rican descent include the understanding that staying silent or imposing silence is unacceptably rude. A discussion in which one of the parties must be silent violates all expectations of a healthy human interaction. When I saw how comfortably my fellow MFA students acquiesced to the gag rule, I felt that I was in a profoundly foreign place.[21]

It could be helpful to view the "gag rule" not just as a social practice but also as a community tradition in the culture of North American CW, especially through the eyes of (international) student-authors who may not be familiar with "Euro-American traditions" of literary evaluation.[22] Acknowledging this tradition as particularly Euro-American, GSIs can look for alternatives to accommodate student-authors emerging from varied environments— whether they be Puerto Rican, Ethiopian, or Japanese. This can occur while skirting ways the normative workshop's "gag rule" alone contradicts both TI principles of *ensuring safety* and *establishing trustworthiness*, thereby avoiding the normative model potentially (re)traumatizing student-authors from minoritized/marginalized backgrounds like Morales Kearns's.[23]

In other words, any attempt to critique the dimensions of the normative workshop must also address the workshop's social dimensions. This is done through pedagogical strategies that can't just aim to change what the workshop is and does, but must also instruct student-authors in manners of navigating difference and privilege in the workshop itself, as well as the workshop's reading materials. Since the workshop may be presented to some, as it had been to Morales Kearns, as a "distinctly raced practice," a first step toward a nonnormative model fused with a TI approach might involve incorporating antiracist practices into the workshop space.

*        *        *

It might be easy enough to identify our pandemic timeline as the one that brought us here. Especially with the overlap of George Floyd's murder, common and widespread dialogue about racism and antiracism has taken place alongside dialogues focused on health (in)equity and what persistently racist spaces look like, as well as how nonwhite people get treated in these spaces. Not exempt from these discussions are CW educators and student-authors who attempt their best work in spaces that install invisible barriers based on racialized thought and behavior.

I try to begin with my student-authors by encouraging them to discern between *racism* and *racial prejudice*. For example, we might discuss how a white person who hates a nonwhite person is perhaps not *racist*, but that a white person who hates a nonwhite person is *racially prejudiced*. We'd cover that someone white who hates a nonwhite person or people *and* works at a bank, however, and who denies a nonwhite person a loan, may be racist. This could be similar to how a white property manager who denies a nonwhite person housing may also be racist or a white doctor who ignores a nonwhite patient's complaints about pain may be racist. We try clearly emphasizing in the class community that *racism* requires an intersection of prejudice and power.[24]

Felicia Rose Chavez and Matthew Salesses, two figures this discussion shouldn't be without, help shift attention toward the relationship between prejudice and power more specifically in the context of CW pedagogies. Both authors help us consider how CW educators can and should treat student-authors; and they help us think about how classroom management and design overall might be evaluated to better ensure that neither classroom management nor design is racist in practice.

To start with Chavez, an antiracist resource for GSIs can then come from *The Anti-Racist Writing Workshop: How to Decolonize the Creative Classroom* (2021) in which Chavez, a CW educator, explores decolonial and antiracist strategies within her workshops—attuned toward helping student-authors feel that workshops are healthy, dialogic communities that serve as environments for student-authors' own growth. For one thing, Chavez notes that

[p]eople of color need a collaborative artistic community to which they belong and feel safe; they need it, but they don't always know how to ask for it and are often unaware that alternatives exist. It's our responsibility as workshop leaders to verbalize our anti-racist agenda for them, in clear, unapologetic language, language that opens doors instead of closes them. We must reach out to people of color, openly differentiate our approach to the writing workshop, and then welcome them into our collective.[25]

I enjoy the idea that CW educators must "openly differentiate our approach to the writing workshop" so that nonwhite student-authors don't merely enter workshops that feel as though they're yet another clone of one they've taken before. Particularly in nonfiction, it seems helpful for student-authors to be able to know and trust that these workshops' approaches can help them focus on (1) composing new texts/media centered on their experiences and the subjects on which they want to reflect and/or (2) extending the work they've already done, especially when working toward a kind of collection or capstone project. For nonwhite student-authors, it really must be established that this is work they can be encouraged to do by locating a class community "to which they belong and feel safe," which can be a benefit of educators applying a TI approach to the workshop.

I also think about Chavez noting the needs of nonwhite student-authors, which reminds me of a conversation with a colleague once about our shared experiences of teaching at an urban two-year college where students constantly attempted to balance life and coursework expectations. We covered that some students experienced houselessness and some experienced miscarriages or cancer diagnoses, and I feel as though about 90 percent of the time, when these conversations would emerge from students, they did come from those who were nonwhite.

Maybe these students learned that their ability to balance work and life was more nuanced and layered than they'd initially set out believing when enrolling in courses. There might also be a slight matter here of impact bias, with students thinking their diagnosis, their new living situation, and so on, might've taken some adjustment but ultimately wouldn't interrupt their workflow—only to then learn this was far from the truth. In my experience, the notion that nonwhite students were reaching out for these conversations more often than white students indicates for me how much they *do* approach the class community as a space where trust and camaraderie are established— as avenues toward creative, professional, and personal development all at once.

Alongside Chavez's work, another antiracist CW resource includes Matthew Salesses's *Craft in the Real World: Rethinking Fiction Writing and Workshopping* (2021). Salesses discusses relationships between student-authors' cultural values, the ways they compose their work, and whom they imagine (or don't imagine) to be their readers. Though Salesses's book mostly focuses on fiction, there are takeaways applied in general to the normative workshop—especially toward reconsidering how the normative workshop might occur for student-authors participating in nonfiction courses. For instance, Salesses notes that

> [w]hen the "traditional" creative writing workshop, in which the author submits a manuscript to a group of peers and listens silently, began at Iowa, it was developed with shared assumptions in mind. The workshop was made

up of white males reading white male fiction, as students and especially as instructors. In this world only does the "gag rule" make some sense, in that it forced men used to being heard to stop and listen to their likely audience. But the world has moved on. The traditional workshop does not work without shared assumptions. [. . .] Non-normative experience becomes exoticized or unspecific, something extra rather than something foundational.[26]

This reminds me of a class session when student-authors and I discussed race, craft, and literature. I asked them to take a moment to note who they thought the "top-10 most famous authors of all time" were; after they made their lists, I told them to take yet another moment to try paying attention to how many of the authors who showed up on their lists were white. We shared these lists, and it seemed that probably around 7/10 of the authors included weren't just white but were also men.

This led to discussing how much influence from certain literature there'd been on our own understandings of CW practices, and how such influence propels the ways we critique and evaluate readings in the CW classroom. In a course with so much nonfiction focused on identity, it also seemed pertinent to highlight what had always been presented as "mainstream" to us, as opposed to what "becomes exoticized or unspecific" (Salesses). This led to questions like "Why is it that probably everyone in this class has read Shakespeare, but not Maya Angelou?"

At the beginning of a course, as part of our ice-breaking conversations I often ask student-authors to name at least one "mentor text" (a text they recognize as being one they'd like to learn from toward developing their own craft senses) as well as a text they can "culturally relate" to. This gets a dialogue going around which authors/texts we model our work on as we practice CW, whether those models do share our cultural/subcultural aspects or not. This highlights discussions around craft, especially in those instances where our own craft choices are culturally (rather than just aesthetically) informed.

My workshops also tend to place the student-author front and center rather than decenter them. This is in part due to class caps for courses at my home institution (19 students) but regardless of enrollment I often begin the process of workshopping student-authors' work in groups rather than within a full-class context. In a perfect world, I'd have a class of sixteen and could split student-authors into four workshop groups and then spend class time workshopping one student per group per week for a month. This offers the opportunity to enact a sense of engaged pedagogy by working closely with student-authors within the intimacy of small groups, rather than having student-authors' questions/ anxieties be drowned out by all the voices in a class community of almost twenty. I find this workshop approach gives student-authors more opportunity to consider their relationship to audience(s). Because they engage in a back-and-forth with a small audience (i.e., the class community) who has read their work, they get to think through dialoguing about whom their revised draft might target (and whether their initial draft targeted anyone in the first place) and how these considerations offer a sense of agency over the direction their work goes.

Finally, we can be encouraged here to consider how, as Salesses notes, "if we are to use workshop as a pedagogical approach, we need to actively acknowledge and confront the dangers of workshop both to the writing itself—if 'writing itself' even exists—and to our personhoods."[27] Especially in nonfiction, the idea of "confront[ing] the dangers of workshop" to "our personhoods" contains potential risk for student-authors when they've focused on experiences their peers must be encouraged to believe (rather than reject) in order for there to be useful feedback toward revision. This isn't only connected to their work but is also connected to their frame of experience: it can be so easy for a nonfiction student-author to feel that a rejection of their work is a rejection of themselves; so, educators must remind them that their experiences are valid when voiced. By merely validating student-authors' experiences alongside them, educators and student-authors can collaboratively discern how to more clearly articulate experiences toward unknowing audiences.

## Praxis

Holding discussions around the potentially traumatizing parameters of the CW classroom while also trying to avoid (re)traumatization in nonfiction workshops can involve GSIs executing nonnormative models that explicitly address the workshop's affect/emotional dimensions. This could not only allow GSIs to *maximize collaboration* and *prioritize empowerment* around discussions of social violence while in the CW class community but also *establish trustworthiness* between and among student-authors from minoritized/marginalized positions who might be apprehensive about these very discussions. For instance, while my own white student-authors are often just as hesitant to explicitly discuss race in their writing as young cisgender men students are to discuss "women's issues," I routinely see student-authors who are nonwhite and who aren't cis young men be perhaps even eager to do so—pulling me toward a need to prepare the whole class community for these discussions, regardless of our racialized and gendered identities.

To begin with traumatic aspects of racialization, acknowledging *racial trauma* (also identified as RBTS/Race-Based Traumatic Stress, defined as "the mental and emotional injury caused by encounters with racial bias and ethnic discrimination, racism, and hate crimes") with student-authors can prepare them for how experiences of RBTS can show up in their writing.[28] This includes subjects like language discrimination (being commanded, for instance, to "speak English") or international students having been told to "go back to [their] country" by an off-campus stranger.

To formally prepare student-authors to discuss race in the class community, a helpful first project in one of my courses has been adapted from David Mura's "Assignment 2: Exploring Your Identity," which can potentially be broken up into different projects (or different components of the same project). I begin with one option as a flash nonfiction project—the premise coming from Mura to "[w]rite about the first time you became aware of or discovered your racial identity."[29] This also ties to Mura's broader prompt, which instructs student-authors to keep a notebook in which "[t]he subject of this notebook is 'you.' Your identity. Your racial and ethnic identity. And any other ways you choose to identify yourself—gender, sexuality, class, region, country, family, immigrant, and so on."[30] Much like first-year composition (FYC) courses in the United States often ask student-authors to explore themselves through expressive writing, an assignment/project like Mura's can help nonfiction student-authors explore/examine their racialized and ethnic identities almost right from the start. Overall, this "Identity Notebook" option encourages student-authors to begin examining themselves, their life histories, and their family histories within a larger web of geography, history, politics, and additional negotiations of identity.

The result might be (A) getting student-authors to be more comfortable with the prospect of discussing race with one another (resulting in *ensuring safety, establishing trustworthiness, maximizing collaboration, prioritizing empowerment*) in a TI classroom setting, hopefully mitigating any trauma(s) elicited through dialogue about student-authored texts and the racialized experiences in those texts. And (B) if the whole class becomes encouraged to discuss race (nonwhite and white class community members alike), this can also work to prepare the class community for the possibility of multiple and varied discussions around racialized identities and experiences.

As a deeper part of the exercise (or perhaps as a different assignment/project altogether), Mura also asks student-authors to pursue the questions: "Who am I? Who are my people? What history led to and produced me? What is the history I never learned that I need to know in order to know who I am? What is my buried history? What is the buried history of my people? My family? My country?"[31] This harbors potential to move in directions of different lengths: In one manner, student-authors can figure out how to compose meditative/ exploratory nonfiction work pursuing the foregoing questions; in another manner, pursuing this inquiry might even expand into something book-length. Especially when one explores "the history of [their] people" there's always, no matter our backgrounds, so much history to uncover and, of course, questions to pursue about the relationships between race, geography, language, and so on—a history that keeps unfolding as these questions continue to be explored in our writing.

I did begin this inquiry with student-authors myself, letting them know that were I to pursue Mura's assignment as an author I'd begin with my multiracial heritage and identity. I'd begin with my grandparents. To start, my maternal grandmother's mother was Black, while her father had a Chahta (Choctaw) mother and a biracial Black-Acadian father. Both of my maternal grandfather's parents were biracial: his mother was Chikasha (Chickasaw) and white Portuguese, while his father was Black and white Irish. Then, on my father's side, my grandmother had a biracial Black and German-Jewish mother, and a Haitian father. Finally, my paternal grandfather's mother was Mvskoke Creek, while his father was Black and white Irish.

I've shared this information with student-authors to get their feet wet with the exercise of writing about their own racialized and ethnic heritages. After providing my family background, I asked that they begin writing out all they know about their own biological grandparents—which might turn into discussing who their great-grandparents were, whether there's any connection to immigration, whether there's any connection to African enslavement and so on, using this to pursue more questions about their relatives' places in history. It's helpful to remind student-authors that everyone in the class community has ancestors and that, as part of our investigative work, we can consider where our ancestors are placed on different points along a historical timeline.

In US history, at least, it can be difficult to discuss history without also talking about war. But it can be useful to ask student-authors, *What were your relatives doing during World War II or during the American Civil War? Or (beyond war) What were your relatives doing during the Great Depression? Were your relatives in the United States during these events—and if not, where were they instead, and what were they doing? What were your relatives up to throughout transatlantic enslavement?* And more. These very questions once led me to a conversation with a student-author whose paternal side is entirely Greek, and so we discussed tracing their ethnic heritage back to ancient Greece and circumventing US history altogether, overall broadening the kind of geography and timeline this student-author could operate on in their work.

Ideally, this all translates to nobody being particularly shocked by any one student-author's submission of a text centering race to full-class or (*maximizing choice*) small-group workshop. Frankly, especially for white student-authors, it encourages discussions of racialized identity through the lenses of history and heritage, which tries to work toward getting us all on the same page of considering heritage rather than placing heritage/ancestry within a hierarchy (e.g., white supremacy). It attempts to do the work of discussing race and racialization without accusing any one student-author of racialized prejudice, instead aiming for a sense of comfort in the class community recognizing, regardless of our ethnic and racialized backgrounds, that we can begin conversations about race in ways that, through nonfiction, initially offer access to learning about ourselves.

Finally, I hope student-authors can carry these discussions toward projects/ exercises that allow them to be proud of what they learn. A potential hurdle I discuss with student-authors is that, while there's always much that we can (or perhaps do) know about our family histories, there's also and always much we don't know. In some instances, student-authors are adopted; other times, like for myself, Black student-authors are completely ignorant of their ancestral African history. For these student-authors, one route we might take is to make our processes a matter of curiosity—on top of having student-authors write what they do know they can also (or instead) write about what they don't know or what they wish they knew. This can grow into a form of writing attached to self-exploration and inquiry—especially when self-exploration is tied to something as potentially complex as racialized identity.

This work reminds me of Jenny Boully's essay "On the EEO Genre Sheet" wherein Boully writes about how, because her father was adopted, what he knows about his ethnic history/heritage is somewhat limited. As Boully puts it, "[m]y father grew up knowing only that he was half Cherokee, half white. We've never known where his white ancestors came from; he became a ward of the state when he was eight, and so much of his history was lost."[32] I love providing an essay like Boully's for student-authors to write about racialized identity, because it's helpful for nonwhite and white student-authors alike through allowing all involved in reading the essay to consider potential complications around the knowledge that surrounds family histories. And while being willing, able, and open to talking about all this won't solve all issues of racism, racial prejudice, or white supremacy in the classroom, it does hopefully shift our affective positions toward discussing racialized identity in the class community. Especially in CW spaces where nonfiction student-authors often incorporate work centralizing their racialized identities, this does and should serve as an open invitation for all involved to practice the ways we can discuss race by way of creative writing.

\* \* \*

Unfortunately, toward reforming the CW workshop, antiracism is not enough. For student-authors whose nonfiction focuses on experiences of sexual violence, GSIs can remain helpful to them by recognizing that such experiences might show up in student-authored writing and that a TI approach to discussing this writing can help student-authors avoid regret at having shared this writing in the first place. This runs counter to a trauma-specific approach wherein student-authors are asked by the instructor to compose writing about their sexually violent/traumatic experiences to "work through" them—rather, it operates by maintaining openness toward a space where these experiences may be shared (*ensuring safety, establishing trustworthiness, and maximizing choice*) openly and without judgment or criticism.

One resource for GSIs to explore might be Penni Russon's "Beyond Trigger Warnings: Working Towards a Strength-Based, Trauma-Informed Model of Resilience in the University Creative Writing Workshop," where Russon notes that "[w]hile the writer's workshop in the university is not a therapeutic space, it is not a place of emotional neutrality."[33] Russon champions a "competence, autonomy, and relatedness triad" that "boosts the effectiveness and enjoyment of the class, while helping students achieve long-term goals."[34] This "triad" could be helpful toward considering how to help student-authors work beyond anxieties around difficult conversations centering traumatic experiences in their writing or in class discussion. Russon's triad allows for student-authors to work toward their strengths rather than having the workshop prey on their fears, helping them produce work that, at the end of the day, they can be prouder of.

Russon concludes that "[e]xploring the ways in which students experience 'safety' and 'risk' in the writer's workshop, may help workshop facilitators engage vulnerable students and help more students meet their short and long-term goals."[35] This makes me think CW educators might need to preface more conversations at the beginning of the term around notions of safety and risk in the class community—there are often things that show up in workshops that neither the student-author nor the educator can fully anticipate in course planning. These prefacing conversations could even be established by way of a "general content warning" on a course syllabus that's forthcoming about what student-authors may encounter throughout a given course.[36] For example, the (university-drafted) statement included on my syllabi looks like what follows:

[b]ecause of the nature of the topics in this class (lived experiences of prejudice, discrimination, abuse, oppression, etc.) the course readings or discussions may generate intellectual and/or emotional discomfort. These responses are natural parts of intellectual growth. If, however, your response becomes acute psychological distress (triggering) then please communicate with me. I invite you to contact me if you have concerns in this regard.

Communicating this to student-authors at the beginning of the school term ideally opens the door to questions they may have about what'll be read and discussed throughout the course—in addition to what gets paired with distributing the course schedule to the class community. As a matter of informed consent, I distribute my syllabus and calendar to prospective students about a week before the term starts as well as a packet of course documents (assignment prompts, rubrics, etc.) to give them a fuller view of what they've signed up for. Striving toward fuller transparency allows student-authors a glimpse at the whole semester; they can get a preview, at the very least, of the kinds of work they'll be engaged with as readers, which allows them to decide how they might pursue the work they want to compose throughout their time in the class.

*   *   *

In "Should Creative Writing Courses Teach Ways of Building Resilience?" Carolyn Jess-Cooke also explores "contemporary practices in using creative writing in recovery from mental illness to consider ways in which undergraduate and postgraduate creative writing programmes might integrate resilience-building techniques for those students who may find some writing exercises 'triggering' or detrimental to their mental health," also arguing that "resilience techniques might enable students to manage 'raw' material and personal narratives in a positive way, and therefore become better creative writers."[37] I'm interested in this approach first because Jess-Cooke's title is a question, and because this description offers an openness toward exploration. There's no immediate *yes* or *no* about whether resilience holds a place in CW pedagogies, so it's helpful to view how this approach can take student-authors' mental health positions within CW class communities into consideration— especially given the personal narratives and "raw material" that might appear in a workshop space, it seems important to remain open to the *should* around the relationship between resilience and CW pedagogies.

Jess-Cooke notes that resilience techniques come about "as a vital means of supporting the student not only as s/he unconsciously or consciously mines his or her subconscious, memories and life experience whilst writing, but s/he is exposed to potentially triggering work by other students."[38] I (re)purpose this most directly toward the nonfiction workshop since it contains much "conscious" and "subconscious" work: "conscious" knowledge finds a place in the pages of work student-authors submit, while "subconscious" knowledge is also brought to the fore with the questions student-authors' peers and/or instructors might ask during a workshop session. It may be equally important to add to this the possibility that student-authored work can elicit conscious and subconscious thought from peers as audience members; so, Jess-Cooke's question/exploration can be just as helpful for student-authors who *want* to write about difficult experiences. (This might also be helpful for peers who become unexpectedly upset by their classmates' writing.)

Regarding how Jess-Cooke intends to address this, they propose a pedagogy that integrates resilience with creative writing borrows from progressivist, student-centric models, as well as Stephanie Vanderslice's research on metacognitive reflection (Vanderslice 2012) and [Celia] Hunt's notion of "transformative learning." There are three key areas in which resilience is most important and/or can be developed in creative writing courses:

(1) workshops, where reading other student's work may prove upsetting for a student, or indeed the act of receiving criticism from other students on work that is highly personal and emotionally drawn

(2) writing exercises, frequently used during my seminars, where there is opportunity to facilitate cognitive development

(3) those parts of the course which are devoted to the "business" of writing, whereby the realities of rejection—and the distress that can follow the rejection of highly personal work—can be positively addressed.[39]

This layout is helpful in that parts of the discussion must be pointed concretely toward (1) workshop, (2) class writing, and (3) the possible (in)advertent rejection of a student-author's quite personal nonfiction. This can coalesce into ways a course design may sneakily encourage student-authors to practice resilience techniques without the educator even needing to use a word like *resilience* in classrooms at all. Such a trajectory points toward the possibility that student-authors can fortify their relationship to difficult writing—not through the educator stating something like "I'm going to make you stronger" but, rather, having student-authors discover their own strength through the course's design in the first place.

In terms of workshops, Jess-Cooke reports having student-authors use written journals wherein they write about how they respond to their peers' work:

This dual-response system—shifting between written feedback which is intended to offer constructive criticism for classmates and a journal for personal reflection—is intended to develop students' cognitive development, enhancing their self-awareness of emotional responses as readers. The journal offers an important way of recording responses to their own creative writing submissions to the workshop, and permits a method of reflective appreciation and implementing feedback.[40]

I've never taken part in a workshop that *required* a journal, so this would be a novel approach for me. I imagine that if I were to implement this in class it might go over similarly to when I ask students in non-CW courses to keep reading and research journals. Whether they do so in Google Docs or composition notebooks, students reflect in their notebooks on what they've read (which I read without assigning a grade; I only check to see that their journal develops/that the number of pages they've written grows).

If CW educators might imagine journals in a nonfiction course where difficult experiences can be discussed, this might then be a way to better "check in" with student-authors. This could involve reading notebook/journal entries and asking student-authors whether they'd like to conference based on what they've written—I've never had to do this, but the idea of using a journal in a nonfiction course evokes possibilities for talking with student-authors outside the class community, toward discerning what they might need from me as their instructor and figuring out how they might wish to navigate this territory with their peers in class. It can be helpful if Student X says, for instance, "Student Y wrote this, and it made me feel this way," because I can then ask, "How would you like to move forward?"

On resilience and rejection, then, Jess-Cooke notes how

> [r]ejection can be catastrophic for those writers who have not developed sufficient emotional resilience or who have failed to regard their work as separate from their identity. In my experience as a student, the "business" of creative writing involved crafting letters to agents and publishers, or speaking with editors about market trends—and yet a major element of this "business" is dealing with the often dramatic shifts that occur between investing emotionally in a creative piece and making it a public, and perhaps commercial, enterprise. Classroom-based discussion of these shifts has been particularly helpful for my own students, as has drawing upon the science world in enabling writers to re-conceptualise "failure" and "rejection." Scientists conduct experiments with the expectation that a high percentage will fail. A similarly experimental approach to writing—alongside cognitive recognition of the emotional contexts of creative writing "experiments"— may serve students very well when it comes to publishing their work.[41]

An approach like this for me would require that I treat my courses differently than I do. My CW courses do have a "professional" aspect to them in that I often have student-authors *prepare* projects for submission—unlike Jess-

Cooke, though, I don't require that they submit anything for publication. Instead, I look over their cover letter drafts, I examine how/whether their prepared submission aligns itself with their chosen publication (whether it's an appropriate fit or not). I feel it's better to provide student-authors options, rather than require them to make their work public outside the class community.

Working on professionalization in the class community can also help toward letting student-authors decide whether they're ready. I don't need to push them toward publishing because they can decide this for themselves, so any discussion about rejection might just need to be paired with discussion about possibility—for example, the possibility that student-authors will send work out on their own terms. Keeping this a possibility rather than a requirement is also much more in line with how I've come to understand a TI approach to CW pedagogies.

To conclude a note on resilience techniques, Jess-Cooke writes that

[o]f course, resilience is difficult to assess, and the intended outcomes—increased esteem, self-confidence, the ability to give feedback in a classroom where material may be triggering, the ability to work through the "murky waters" of the subconscious in a positive manner—are tricky to measure. But given the popularity of creative writing courses and the highly personal manner in which students approach the discipline, it would seem that an address of resilience is necessary in creative writing programmes. Further research remains to be done into the benefits of "therapeutic" approaches within creative writing programmes and pedagogy; however, a model which allows the student-writer to engage cognitively with the self on the page, and which prioritises the wellbeing and cognitive development of the writer will facilitate empowerment and better writing.[42]

I do believe it's beyond the scope of this chapter to envision the *measurability* and *assessment* of how teaching resilience techniques in CW might play out, especially if, as Jess-Cooke notes, we need further research about "therapeutic" approaches to this matter. What I suggest should be part of the forward movement in the discussions around resilience in CW class communities might focus on how educators can decide where *they* fit: If part of the discussion is meant to be about how CW educators can prepare themselves to be "resilient" in the face of student-authored writing, they might follow their own advice to student-authors through their own teaching journals, through check-ins with other GSIs/faculty, through university-provided counseling, and so on. GSIs might talk with the faculty of their respective programs about how to prepare for coverage of difficult material in the class community. Overall, I don't pretend to have solutions for what GSIs *should* do, so instead I return to the modal verb in Jess-Cooke's title.

*    *    *

A final resource for this discussion involving GSIs preparing themselves for difficult classroom dialogues is Krista Ratcliffe's "Rhetorical Listening: A Trope for Interpretive Invention and a 'Code of Cross-Cultural Conduct,'" where Ratcliffe covers *rhetorical listening* as a way to foster a cross-cultural dialogue in ways that result in reception and invention, rather than resistance and denial—which is crucial toward gathering the perspectives of those with worldviews and frames of reference/experience different from our own.

This is especially important when these relate to "cultural categories" such as "age and class, nationality and history, religion and politics."[43] To explore these, Ratcliffe asks questions like

> [w]hy is it so hard to listen to one another? Why is it so hard to resist a guilt/blame logic when we do listen? Why is it so hard to identify with one another when we feel excluded? Why is it so hard to focus simultaneously on commonalities and differences among ourselves? And how do the power differentials of our particular standpoints influence our ability to listen?[44]

When pursued in CW class communities, these questions help us locate new angles for evaluating (especially) nonfiction from geographies and cultures different from those we're familiar with as readers. This extends not just to whatever published nonfiction might be encountered in class but also includes the nonfiction shared between student-authors as peers. It's important for them to be able to "resist a guilt/blame logic" while attempting to "focus simultaneously on commonalities and differences among ourselves"—this can encourage student-authors to hold generative conversations that don't necessarily run the risk of one shutting another down when certain experiences are written about, or because the student-author can't understand another's frame of reference/experience.

Ratcliffe also notes that

[b]y championing a responsibility logic, not a guilt/blame one, rhetorical listening offers us the possibility of getting past the guilt/blame tropes of accusation, denial, and defensiveness—all of which are associated with authorial intent and all of which usually result in a stalemate that preserves the status quo. By championing a responsibility logic, rhetorical listening asks us, first, to judge not simply the person's intent but the historically situated discourses that are (un)consciously swirling around and through the person and, second, to evaluate politically and ethically how these discourses function and how we want to act upon them.[45]

This can help us consider why, for example, a nonwhite student-author might wish to write explicitly about racialized experiences. Or, why a woman or immigrant may wish to write about experiences of gendered or language-based social violence. This opens us (ideally) to notions not just of "authorial intent" but also of exigence, namely those (sometimes deeply personal) reasons why student-authors compose certain nonfiction material in class. Ideally, envisioning these exigencies can help explore what's so often referred to in writing classrooms as the "So what?" question: The question around parts of a text that a classroom audience might ask a student-author to articulate in workshop toward providing a clearer sense of the student-author's aims in their draft as well as with any goals for successive revision.

Finally, it's helpful that Ratcliffe notes how rhetorical listening "turns intent back on the listener, focusing on listening with intent, not for it" as well as that it "turns the meaning of the text into something larger than itself, certainly larger than the intent of the speaker/writer, in that rhetorical listening locates a text as part of larger cultural logics."[46] This encourages student-authors to consider how their and their peers' texts might perform as cultural artifacts—not just as products of their creativity or expression but as ways to foster conversations about the many subjects that get covered in the personal essay, literary journalism, memoir, and much more that appears within a nonfiction curriculum.

This serves as an invitation toward rhetorical and active listening that can foster the workshop space as a class community—in doing so, the space can perform as trauma-informed through a focus on contexts that are inclusive not just of student-authored products, but student agency and the search for answers to "So what?"

# Conclusions

As Janice Carello and Lisa D. Butler further remind us in "Potentially Perilous Pedagogies: Teaching Trauma Is Not the Same as Trauma-Informed Teaching," although educators who engage in trauma-specific praxis "appear to appreciate some of the force and significance of traumatic experience, their practice does not reflect an understanding of the implications of trauma, retraumatization, or secondary traumatization for student adjustment and academic performance."[47] For this reason I stress that GSIs learning to conduct their CW workshops (if they even wish for their courses to remain a workshop) must, on top of maintaining CW courses as nonnormative, ensure that they're trauma-informed. The GSI has a sort of dual task in allowing for freedom and flexibility (already part of the TI framework) on the part of student-authors getting to write in ways they feel can help themselves. At the same time, GSIs must do the best they can to reduce the risk of potential (re)traumatization/ vicarious traumatization on student-authors' part in nonfiction courses and on GSIs' own parts—any of whom may have also survived traumatic experiences. As Carello and Butler note, "[a]s educators we undoubtedly need to teach about trauma; at the same time, we must also *be mindful of how we teach it* as well as how we teach trauma survivors."[48]

Even though assertions like Carello's and Butler's might mostly be helpful for composing practices in fiction they can be applied to nonfiction, too, especially through discussions around importing writing practices into pedagogies where student-authors become expected to consider their authorial choices. Student-authors can, in the process, ask questions like the ones seen in this chapter, not just while writing but also during their prewriting, to place them a step ahead when preparing work for their target audience(s).

Finally, as Janelle Adsit notes in *Toward an Inclusive Creative Writing: Threshold Concepts to Guide the Literary Curriculum* (2017) CW "demands a thorough consideration of audience," which may also connect to Adsit's and my shared belief that "the onus is on the creative writing curriculum to expand the terms of reference that a writer can engage, so that they can move between different audiences."[49] As a result, CW curricula have "more than one reason to teach cross-cultural competency and humility" and so the notion of encouraging student-authors to think about moving "between different audiences" can prod more thoughtfulness overall around the composing choices within their texts.[50]

This leads GSIs down a certainly formidable path. It's an admirable path, nonetheless, recognizing that GSIs, especially those who themselves come into their first teaching classrooms attempting to cover nonfiction with potentially difficult content, do so knowing they also do their best to create classrooms that foster their own student-authors' senses of safety—knowing they foster senses of growth. Senses of having learned not just more about themselves as authors but about the world(view)s their peers enter the class community to share.

## Writing Prompts

1. Draft a set of outcomes (e.g., "In this workshop, we'll . . .") for a community nonfiction workshop of your design. Detail how you hope community members can benefit from participating, as well as how they can practice (creative) nonfiction writing in the community itself.
2. Draft nonfiction media meant deliberately for public display. Will this take the form of a video? An audio essay? A large canvas? Images projected onto a wall? Finally, how might community members respond as they engage with the form you've chosen?
3. After George Orwell's essay "Why I Write," title your draft "For Whom Do I Write?" Begin with this title. Mention a geographic location.

## Notes

1   "Writers' Workshop." *History | Iowa Writers' Workshop*, College of Liberal Arts & Sciences | The University of Iowa, https://writersworkshop.uiowa.edu/about/about-workshop/history.
2   I want to mention as immediately as I can here my late discovery of Renee Linklater's *Decolonizing Trauma Work: Indigenous Stories and Strategies* (2014). I wasn't familiar with Linklater's book until after many drafts of this chapter—I mention it in this note as a way for us to consider trauma and resilience beyond white and Western recognitions of trauma, "mental illness," and "mental health." In another version of this chapter, Linklater's work would receive a grand amount of attention.
3   Nguyen, Beth. "Unsilencing the Writing Workshop." *Literary Hub*, April 15, 2019, https://lithub.com/unsilencing-the-writing-workshop.

4   Ibid.

5   Ibid.

6   Murray, Sabina and Ocean Vuong. "How Can We Make the MFA Workshop More Hospitable to Writers of Color?" *Literary Hub*, April 4, 2019, https://lithub .com/how-can-we-make-the-mfa-workshop-more-hospitable-to-writers-of -color.

7   Ibid.

8   Carello, Janice and Lisa D. Butler. "Practicing What We Teach: Trauma-Informed Educational Practice." *Journal of Teaching in Social Work*, vol. 35, no. 3, 2015, pp. 262–78.

9   Ibid., p. 264.

10  Ibid., p. 267.

11  Ibid., p. 264.

12  Also see: Molloy, Cathryn. "Multimodal Composing as Healing: Toward a New Model for Writing as Healing Courses." *Composition Studies*, vol. 44, no. 22, 2016, pp. 134–52, https://www.jstor.org/stable/2485933.

13  "Trauma-specific nonfiction pedagogy" could be a quite helpful exploration outside the scope of this chapter, and it's one I encourage readers to pursue, should they have the appropriate interdisciplinary training/background.

14  At the time of this writing, according to RAINN (the Rape, Abuse & Incest National Network), the overall percentage of US students who experience rape or sexual assault "through physical force, violence, or incapacitation" stands at 13 percent, discerned to be approximately 26 percent for college-aged (18–24) cisgender women, 23 percent for genderqueer students, and 6.8 percent for cisgender men (all within the same age range). Because these statistics overlap with the common/"traditional" ages of student-authors in undergraduate nonfiction courses, it feels most pertinent here to focus on Bethany One's experiences, and on Lindner's approaches toward working with a student-author in this particular case.

15  Lindner, Vicki. "The Tale of Two Bethanies: Trauma in the Creative Writing Class." *New Writing: The International Journal for the Practice and Theory of Creative Writing*, vol. 1, no. 1, 2004, pp. 6–14.

16  Ibid., p. 10.

17  Ibid.

18  Ibid., pp. 12–13.

19  Morales Kearns, Rosalie. "Voice of Authority: Theorizing Creative Writing Pedagogy." *College Composition and Communication*, vol. 60, no. 4, 2009, pp. 790–807.

20  GSIs can also refer to Beth Nguyen's "Unsilencing the Writing Workshop."

21  Morales Kearns, p. 794.

22  Also see Natasha Sajé's "The Politics of Literary Evaluation."

23  Beyond issues of workshop silencing, another layer inherent to the normative workshop being positioned as a Euro-American tradition might involve understanding how it has operated as an academic tradition of fault-finding—as such, it has remained a way of evaluating writing itself. If this is indeed the basis for the normative workshop, it's GSIs' responsibility to then divert from this mode and instead consider ways to deliver options (maximizing choice) to student-authors who, like Rosalie Morales Kearns, don't come to the workshop from the same tradition(s) the workshop itself does, and who may also internalize both silencing and error-correction as (re)traumatizing educational modes.

24  As Yawo Brown delineates this in "The Subtle Linguistics of Polite White Supremacy": "Racism is the systemic oppression of one group of people who can be categorized within certain phenotypical traits over multiple generations that has been, at one point, sanctioned by a country, the majority and/or ruling class." Prejudice, meanwhile, "though harmful, is not necessarily systemic and can be committed by anyone. It simply requires one to pre-judge. It does not require its user to have any access to the ruling class or status of whiteness" (Brown n. pag.).

25  Chavez, Felicia Rose. *The Anti-Racist Writing Workshop: How to Decolonize the Creative Classroom.* Haymarket Books, 2021.

26  Salesses, Matthew. *Craft in the Real World: Rethinking Fiction Writing and Workshopping.* Catapult, 2021.

27  Ibid., pp. 128–9.

28  Also see Helms, Janet E., et al. "Racism and Ethnoviolence as Trauma: Enhancing Professional Training." *Traumatology*, vol. 18, no. 1, March 2012, pp. 65–74, https://doi.org/10.1177/1534765610396728.

29  Mura, p. 244.

30  Ibid., p. 243.

31  Ibid.

32  Boully, Jenny. *Betwixt-and-Between: Essays on the Writing Life.* Coffee House Press, 2018.

33  Russon, Penni. "Beyond Trigger Warnings: Working Towards a Strengths-Based, Trauma-Informed Model of Resilience in the University Creative Writing Workshop." *TEXT: Journal of Writing and Writing Courses*, vol. 21, 2017, pp. 1–12, https://doi.org/10.52086/001c.25896.

34  Ibid., p. 9.

35  Ibid., p. 10.

36  Also see: Flaherty, Colleen. "New Study Says Trigger Warnings are Useless. Does That Mean They Should be Abandoned?" *Inside Higher Ed*, March 21, 2019, www .insidehighered.com/news/2019/03/21/new-study-says-trigger-warnings-are -useless-does-that-mean-they-should-be-abandoned.

37  Jess-Cooke, Carolyn. "Should Creative Writing Courses Teach Ways of Building Resilience?" *New Writing: The International Journal for the Practice and Theory of Creative Writing*, vol. 12, no. 2, pp. 249–59, https://doi.org/10.1080 /147907262015.1047855.

38  Ibid., p. 254.

39  Ibid., pp. 255–6.

40  Ibid., p. 256.

41  Ibid., p. 257.

42  Ibid.

43  Ibid.

44  Ratcliffe, Krista. "Rhetorical Listening: A Trope for Interpretive Invention and a 'Code of Cross-Cultural Conduct.'" *College Composition and Communication*, vol. 51, no. 2, 1999, pp. 195–224.

45  Ibid., p. 208.

46  Ibid., p. 220.

47  Carello, Janice and Lisa D. Butler. "Potentially Perilous Pedagogies: Teaching Trauma is Not the Same as Trauma-Informed Teaching." *Journal of Trauma & Dissociation*, vol. 15, 2014, pp. 153–68.

48  Ibid., p. 163.

49  Adsit, Janelle. *Toward an Inclusive Creative Writing: Threshold Concepts to Guide the Literary Curriculum*. Bloomsbury Academic, an Imprint of Bloomsbury Publishing Plc, 2017, p. 99.

50  Ibid.

# Further Reading

Biswas, Shampa. "Advice on Advising: How to Mentor Minority Students." *ChronicleVitae*, March 13, 2019, https://chroniclevitae.com/news/2172-advice-on -advising-how-to-mentor-minority-students?cid=VTEVPMSED1.

Brown, Yawo. "The Subtle Linguistics of Polite White Supremacy." *Medium*, August 17, 2015, https://medium.com/@YawoBrown/the-subtle-linguistics-of-polite-white -supremacy-3f83c907ffff.

Dodd, Leanne. "Insider Research: Representing Peripheral Voices and Multiple Identities when Writing about Personal Trauma." *C I N D E R: Creative*

*Innovations & New Directions in Expressive Research*, no. 3, 2020, https://doi.org/10.21153/cinder2020art951.

Exoo, Christian and Sydney Fallone. "Using CNF to Teach the Realities of Sexual Assault to First Responders: An Annotated Bibliography." *Assay: A Journal of Nonfiction Studies*, vol. 2, no. 1, fall 2015, https://www.assayjournal.com/christian-exoo--sydney-fallon-using-cnf-to-teach-the-realities-of-sexual-assault-to-8203first-responders-an-annotated-bibliography65279-21.html.

Islam, Maimuna. "Loosening Our Tongues: Toward a Critical Race Practice in Fiction Writing Workshops." *Pedagogy: Critical Approaches to Teaching Literature, Language, Composition, and Culture*, vol. 17, no. 2, 2017, pp. 289–319.

Laub, Dori. "Bearing Witness or the Vicissitudes of Listening." *The Holocaust: Theoretical Readings*, edited by Neil Levi and Michael Rothberg, Edinburgh University Press, 2003, pp. 221–6, http://www.jstor.org/stable/10.3366/j.ctvxcrd5m.36.

Linklater, Renee. *Decolonizing Trauma Work: Indigenous Stories and Strategies*. Fernwood Publishing Co. Ltd., 2014.

McAbee, Donovan. "Shifting the Power Dynamics in the Creative Writing Workshop: Assessing an Instructor as Participant Model." *New Writing: The International Journal for the Practice and Theory of Creative Writing*, vol. 17, no. 3, 2019, pp. 244–52. https://doi.org/10.1080/14790726.2019.1596959.

McGee, Paul. "The Links between Creative Writing and Traumatic Thought." *New Writing: The International Journal for the Practice and Theory of Creative Writing*, vol. 19, no. 1, 2021, pp. 27–37. https://doi.org/10.1080/14790726.2021.1891259.

Mura, David. "White Writing Teachers (or David Foster Wallace vs. James Baldwin)." *Journal of Creative Writing Studies*, vol. 1, no. 1, 2016, Article 7, https://scholarworks.rit.edu/jcws/vol1/iss1/7.

Perry, Gaylene. "Art and Trauma: Danger and Dynamics in the Creative Writing Workshop." *Educational Insights*, vol. 11, no. 1, 2007, pp. 1–14.

Rickett, Carolyn and Sue Joseph. "Beyond This Point Here Be Dragons: Consideration and Caution for Supervising HDR Writing Trauma Project." *TEXT Special Issue 42: Writing and Trauma*, edited by Bridget Haylock and Suzanne Hermanoczki, October 2017, http://www.textjournal.com.au/speciss/issue42/content.htm.

Watkins, Claire Vaye. "On Pandering." *Tin House*, 2015, https://tinhouse.com/on-pandering.

# 2

# Writing Lives at the Roundtable

## Toward Teaching Students-as-Authors

Creative writing (CW) educators must reflect on how they display care toward (undergraduate) student-authors by way of attention toward how their senses of authorship become developed. That is, how and in which ways do educators including graduate student instructors (GSIs) take time with their students' authorial development, rather than only the development of "quality work" in CW courses? In pursuing this question, GSIs can emphasize a culturally dexterous framework toward establishing trust between themselves and their CW class communities—another goal being to develop students' authorial senses by re-centering agency, increasing focus on effective peer communication between and among student-authors and educators when coming to the class community from differing backgrounds.

Module 1 for the proposed PACTS curriculum is expressed as "establishing trust in the physician-patient relationship."[1] Though this likely intends to be envisioned in clinical settings, CW pedagogy might also envision centering itself around objectives leading toward established trust, especially in considering student-authors' own backgrounds. In the specific context of CW pedagogy, a culturally dexterous CW outcome might be expressed this way: *In this course, student-authors will establish trust in the creative writing class community, both in peer-to-peer relationships and in the instructor/student-author relationship.*

Questions to pursue might then surround what it can *mean* to establish trust between student-authors, their peers, and CW educators. More pointedly, how might this be done when the course is run by a GSI first learning to teach in CW? Finally, how could student-authors come to practice compassion toward difference in the classroom through GSIs' pedagogical examples?

# Authorial Lives and Constructions

I care about imagining this outcome because I had no clear guide for myself as a student-author, going into CW classrooms bare toward whichever advice my instructors decided to give. "Becoming an author," to me, meant internalizing all the guidance I received through others' CW pedagogies—but without any critical consideration of how authors' livelihoods are so often tethered to their identities and the privileges (or lack thereof) that come with them.

At nineteen I'd sit at a picnic table or on a park bench reading the authors recommended to me (in this case, work by J. D. Salinger, Jack Kerouac, and those like them) without any thought of whether the authors' experiences or identities mirrored my own. It wasn't until much later that I encountered those like James Baldwin and Roland Barthes—whom I eventually came to understand while maturing as a reader would've had a nice effect on my younger self since they were queer men. Maybe to my detriment I spent my late teens/early twenties reading work by so many authors who were white, so many who were straight, and so many who instilled cultural writing senses that played a part not just in my personhood but also my early senses of authorship.

Another objective here might then be to frame student-authors' own culturally mediated identities through ideas of what authorship can mean, and in the process guiding nonfiction GSIs still concretizing their own positionality in the classroom. That is, with many nonfiction student-authors hoping to become essayists, journalists, memoirists, reviewers, etc., it feels important to offer GSIs a framework for discussing what authorship and the "writing life" can mean, as well as how common "advice" about what it means to "become a writer" gets perpetuated throughout CW in North American higher education.

\*   \*   \*

Somewhere to start considering authorial constructions might be through Alice Walker's "Saving the Life That Is Your Own: The Importance of Models in the Artist's Life," wherein Walker considers authorship through advocating for models and patterns that serve important purposes for burgeoning artists. Walker calls the *absence* of these models an "occupational hazard for the artist," noting that "models in art, in behavior, in growth of spirit and intellect—even if rejected—enrich and enlarge one's view of existence."[2] I'm intrigued by how Walker braids modeling in art and life—how she ties modeling to enlarging "one's view of existence." More intriguing is Walker's attention to how modeling gets tethered to an artist's/author's identity, and ways the two might coexist in dissonance.

Walker discovered a model in Zora Neale Hurston. Though, she was lucky: having found someone who could provide her a way to feel represented (reflected, really) in literature and life, Walker was able to rely on Hurston as a model to craft her selfhood, to craft her practice, and to mold her authorial convictions. Many authors must write their work as a trail of crumbs for others to eventually follow. However, as Walker puts it, "as if she knew someday I would come along wandering in the wilderness," Zora Neale Hurston gave her the way toward a writing life that she hadn't seen from anyone else.[3]

When author Toni Morrison, about whom Walker writes in "Saving the Life That Is Your Own," said that she "writes the kind of books she wants to read, [Morrison] was acknowledging the fact that in a society in which 'accepted literature' is so often sexist and racist and otherwise irrelevant or offensive to so many lives," she also asserted that Morrison needed to "do the work of two. She must be her own model as well as the artist attending, creating, learning from, realizing the model, which is to say, herself."[4] When authors like Toni Morrison need to "do the work of two" through a kind of self-designed modeling created out of a dearth of examples (especially serving those student-authors with minoritized/marginalized identities), then the "work of two" ends up embodying the learner and the model at once.[5] And, while the idea of becoming one's own model might be necessary for so many authors in the margins, at some point the ways minoritized/marginalized student-authors (much less toward the development of their authorial identities) need to be addressed, period. As Walker illustrates it: "It should be remembered that, as a black [*sic*] person, one cannot completely identify with a Jane Eyre, or with her creator, no matter how much one admires them."[6]

## Idea and Identity: The Whole Picture

Some of the ways I've tried covering notions of authorship and agency as a CW educator have been through bell hooks's "to gloria, who is she: on using a pseudonym," Sonya Huber's "The Three Words that Almost Ruined Me as a Writer: 'Show, Don't Tell,'" and Taiyon J. Coleman's "The Thenar Space: Writing Beyond Emotion and Experience into Story." I often begin with hooks not just because I'm her superfan but also because she explains how choosing a pseudonym helped lead her toward "greater awareness about the relationship between author, identity, and a text."[7] As a class community we can try to examine how hooks's work helps us consider what "makes" an author—how an author presents themself, as well as how senses of authorship are at times constructed by the genre(s) in which they compose/their choices with form, tone, and "voice." On top of this, we might consider how these may converge to encourage student-authors to think about the kinds of professional selves they want to develop.

It's helpful for student-authors to note how hooks examines her choice to use a pseudonym, having written that she's "often confronted by readers seeking an explanation" and that *bell hooks* "was initially only a name for writing— then [she] began to use it when [she] gave lectures to avoid confusion."[8] hooks continues to explain that using a pseudonym wasn't just a matter of having a selfhood to present in the space of a lecture or a public reading, but that she was conscious of the distinction between idea and identity. hooks notes that when writing her first book, *Ain't I a Woman: Black Women and Feminism* (1981) she confronted the question around her given name, Gloria Watkins, asking, "[h]ow could Gloria find her voice, speak firmly and directly when I was so accustomed to finding veiled ways of expression, abstract, unclear ways? For me, the pseudonym had a very therapeutic function. Through the use of the name bell hooks I was able to claim an identity that affirmed for me my right to speech."[9] This affirming a "right to speech" echoes throughout the experiences of many racialized people in the United States (and especially for racialized women, as hooks notes).

Attaching racist patterns of silencing to the intersection of action, conversation, and "good behavior," hooks adds that "[u]sing the pseudonym was a constant reminder that my ideas were expressions of me but they were not the whole picture," taking care to remind us that her ideas not being "the whole picture" could in effect encourage student-authors to pursue their own cultural/political work based upon their own identities.[10] For example: those student-authors who through their work affirm that all Black lives matter, who thoroughly examine police budgets, who wish to work toward the freedom of Palestine, who affirm that trans women are women (and that trans men are men), and more. In the process, student-authors using CW to name how they engage with ideas could encounter a helpful (and perhaps therapeutic, as it was for hooks) avenue toward placing a part of their selves onto the page.[11]

hooks finally reminds the class community of the cultural and historical reasons to consider how naming can help identify distinctions between work and selfhood, concluding that

> [n]aming is a serious process: It has been of crucial concern for many individuals within oppressed groups who struggle for self-recovery, for self-determination. It has been important for black [*sic*] people in the United States. Think of the many African-American slaves who renamed themselves after emancipation or the use of nicknames in traditional folk communities, where such names act to tell something specific about the bearer. Within many folk traditions globally, among the Inuit, the Australian Aborigines, naming is a source of empowerment, an important gesture in the process of creation. A primacy is given to naming as a gesture that deeply shapes and influences the social construction of self. As in southern African-American folk traditions, a name is perceived as a force that has the power to determine whether or not an individual will be fully self-realized, whether she or he will be able to fulfill their destiny, find their place in the world.[12]

I want to imagine the potential for this in CW as a way for student-authors to perhaps choose a pseudonym in class as "a source of empowerment" and as an avenue toward "shaping and influencing the social construction of a self" (or, in this instance, the construction of authorial senses). This might not be any different from the already expected use of preferred names and pronouns in class communities, so simply asking *What would you like to be called as an author?* could begin creating trust in the communication between the student-author and the rest of the class community. And as Felicia Rose Chavez also puts it in *The Anti-Racist Writing Workshop: How to Decolonize the Creative Classroom* (2021): "[w]e claim names for ourselves and demand that everyone calls us by our names. In claiming names for ourselves, we name that for which we fight."[13] In other words, not only allowing but encouraging student-authors to employ pseudonyms as a CW exercise might inch them closer toward actualizing their authorial senses—knowing they come into a classroom space two or three times a week to inhabit a self that doesn't have to be the exact same self-presentation who lives in their dorm room, does homework in the library, or works a part-time campus job.

Though we haven't always had full-fledged conversations about naming and empowerment, I have seen student-authors choose pseudonyms in my courses. One way to carry this option further might be to deliberately encourage using pseudonyms in CW classes while embarking on the work ahead for the term. Like in "foreign" language classes in high school, college, and so on, this offers access to deliberate expression by way of a name, rather than toward the possibility of silence.

Sonya Huber's "The Three Words That Almost Ruined Me as a Writer" also offers the class community opportunities to question silencing around the pervasive CW advice "show, don't tell," which can potentially be damaging to students' authorial development. As Huber writes in her essay:

> I tell my students "Show *and* tell," and yet even in 2019 I am disturbed by how often they come into my class, having taken fiction first, telling each other in workshop, "Show, don't tell." This is in the water of creative writing pedagogy. And we need to end it, because it leaks between genres and becomes a mantra, the easiest and therefore seemingly the most clear, most unquestionable.[14]

I see this still in 2022, in student-authors' commentary to one another. And so, it seems inherent to normative CW pedagogies, and questioning its oft-repeated nature is one way to discuss with student-authors how they internalize the advice they've been given about how to construct senses of authorship via the texts instructors ask them to compose in CW courses.

Huber concludes by instructing student-authors to

> [d]escribe what you see outside and what you feel inside, and how the scene inside shifts and whirls and changes in your ribcage and in your skull, how chocolate and rain taste and what they remind you of. Feel things. And say them. Tell me everything. Tell me a story. Tell me the truth. Tell me lies. Tell me what you want to say.[15]

This is encouraging for student-authors to see the repeated advice of *telling* contrast with what they may have learned before entering their first CW classes in college. It acts as permission: permission to dialogue, to remember, and to reflect in ways that aren't relegated only to the privileging of scenes and descriptions that are easily and often discussed as staples of "good (creative) writing."

I can be bad with scenes. To be honest, as I learned to move through my academic experiences as a student-author I'd always found more gravitation toward internalizing and reflection (probably evidenced by my having ended up an essayist). I don't really think it was until graduate school that I was encouraged to fully capitalize on these instances of internalization/reflection in the essay form. Within this encouragement, though, I can say that I found confidence in the presentation of an "essayist self." (This wasn't just through the topics/subjects I expressed interest in writing about, but also through the process of learning to connect myself *to* those subjects.)

A final text I've used in class communities toward discussing authorship is Taiyon J. Coleman's essay "The Thenar Space: Writing Beyond Emotion and Experience into Story," where Coleman expresses the goal (and will) to write in the face of opposition from family members—one of whom was an aunt who told Coleman she was "too stupid" to ever become a writer. (Coleman's title also refers to the thenar as the space connecting our index finger and thumb, an area where many of us hold the tools to construct our stories.)

Coleman's essay isn't just about opposition but also about achieving a self-actualization wherein readers can witness an example of someone whose goal isn't just to define but is also to articulate her authorship, noting how difficult this can be when it's also tied to painful memory. As an author, Coleman notes that she

> learned early in my life from the people closest to me, my family members, that writing and being a writer would be an extremely challenging thing for a poor black [*sic*] girl from Chicago to do and be. It's one thing for Frederick Douglass to write about the curse of new knowledge upon acquiring literacy while enslaved, and another thing to actually live, in "free times," and have literacy, and to still have to act against silencing from your family members, society, culture, and institutions as a woman of color. Negative experiences have first and foremost come from my family and the struggles of a belief in myself, struggles affected and compounded, like really high interest on bad debt, by structural cumulative racism and sexism, and it manifests at a micro, individual, level. As a black [*sic*] female writer, I have had to fight against my family, community, self, and institution while writing simultaneously. In this vein, my literary culture is a proud culture of struggling against silencing to result in the power, art, agency, beauty, and self-actualization that comes from speaking, writing in spite of.[16]

I wonder about the effects an essay like Coleman's has on student-authors searching for their own "literary culture"—not just Black women student-authors but also student-authors from racialized identities who might otherwise be able to internalize the concepts of acting "against silencing from your family members, society, culture, and institutions" toward fostering more intersectional conversations in the class community about authors' experiences as they're articulated from their own backgrounds.[17]

Coleman concludes that "[u]ltimately, my goal as a writer is just to produce writing that tells my story and has utility for readers; I want to always connect outside of myself and my world to the equally valuable worlds and experiences of others."[18] I'm a fan of the combination of telling one's story along with one's writing seeking "utility for readers." This can be difficult for an author to envision given how their readership might utilize their words and concepts, while still getting us to potentially bridge gaps between what we hope as authors to refine as we compose with potential reception of the writing on audiences' part. Coleman classifies writing acts as a combination of "craft, empathy, and compassion," which I see as necessary toward envisioning student-authors "coming into their own" in the class while acknowledging that they can do this not only with compassion toward themselves and their experiences but also toward the audience members who'll potentially benefit from what they've attempted wholeheartedly to write.[19]

## GSI Resources

To begin interrogating notions of authorship in CW class communities, GSIs might review Rachel Hennessy's posturing of CW authorship in "Am I No Longer a Writer? 'Universal' Tenets and the Writing/Teaching Self." Hennessy notes that "if we acknowledge creative writing practices as 'personal and cultural,' then we must be wary, as creative writing instructors, of insisting on fixed notions of what a writer looks like."[20] This gets explored through observing "two very common pieces of advice given to young writers: 'write every day' and 'keep a journal.'"[21] It's also compounded with Elizabeth Forbes's model of "intersecting versions of the writer: maker, artist, creator and performer," with Hennessy noting that Forbes's model "provides a means by which teachers of creative writing might speak to, and interrogate meaningfully, the multiplicity of the authorial identity and consider where the student writer sits among these models."[22] This offers GSIs an opportunity to not just reexamine the advice about authorial identity they've received from their previous instructors but also take into deeper consideration the advice they begin dispersing as CW educators.

To discern what it might entail to meaningfully interrogate this, it could help for GSIs to try conflating the above *authorial identity* with an earlier-established term *autobiographical identity*—borrowed here from Romy Clark and Roz Ivanič, who established autobiographical identity in *The Politics of Writing* (1997) as "the identity people bring with them to any act of writing."[23] Clark and Ivanič suggest that the nature of writing is "sociocognitive"—that neither social identity nor cognition should be neglected and that authors are as inseparable from their cultural backgrounds as they are from how these backgrounds influence their thinking. Both *authorial identity* and *autobiographical identity* might be wrapped up together within *authorship* when placed in the context of CW pedagogies, as the latter can emphasize agency over one's rhetorical (a definition of *rhetoric* here being borrowed from Victor Villanueva as "the conscious use of language") choices in composing, accounting, and allowing space for their linguistic, gendered, racialized, and other backgrounds.[24]

To backtrack, Hennessy crucially examines advice like "write every day," noting how this is saturated with gendered and classed expectations around labor and the creation of a "work-life balance" (also remaining careful to note that it's difficult and sometimes impossible, for instance, for those who are parents, especially if they're mothers, to "write every day"). We've seen from throughout the Covid-19 pandemic alone that a shift in labored expectations (plus a divide between women's and men's productivity throughout various households, especially when they're parents) may be incompatible with the daily writing expectations placed onto student- and professional authors.

This also points to income-related expectations around who's able to complete daily writing—one who works a "nine to five," or perhaps multiple jobs, might find it not just difficult to schedule everyday writing time but must also manage any fatigue around their work schedule. Many authors with full-time jobs note in their craft pieces, on panels, in webinars, and so on that they'll only write on weekends or that they'll wake early every morning to do their creative writing before starting work, or they'll attempt to write only at night; it's important to note that none of the these circumstances can be "universal." As a result, everyday writing shouldn't be communicated as necessary for student-authors as though every student-author can manage their circumstances in the same ways.

I'm reminded of my home institution teetering on whether to close for the remainder of the semester during March 2020. I made a "Plan A" with students, as well as a "Plan B," the former involving a return to the classroom after a slightly extended Spring Break, and the latter meaning there'd be no return to in-person learning. When we learned the university would force us to act on "Plan B" I recognized I didn't have equipment up to date enough to work from home (WFH). So, I bought a new laptop and tablet to forge a home office—enacting the privilege of not only having an occupation ripe to WFH but also the financial privilege to prepare myself to do so. In direct contrast, one student at the time expressed anxiety about our "Plan B" because they couldn't afford internet back home in New York City. There was no way for them to complete classwork on anything but their smartphone—and though they did eventually complete their work, this involved negotiating a grand amount of flexibility throughout the process.

This could return to Hennessy's conclusion that "to encourage students to adopt a regime of regular writing seems self-evident and aligns with the greater academic obsession with time-management, schedules and deadlines," adding to this that "it may be reassuring to some student writers that hours a day will transform them into artists, but there should still be space for the accidental and the unexpected, for allowing time amongst the 'rubble of life' where they might, ultimately, find inspiration."[25] It's pertinent to account for the constraints created by "the greater academic obsession with time-management, schedules, and deadlines" not just around how these ask student-authors to enact care in their practices and habits but also around which of these notions might be unintentionally insensitive to the very real needs of a student-author's circumstances.

While it might be advisable to ask, as Hennessy has, "how can we reasonably omit such [writing] advice?"[26] it may be even more crucial to establish trust in our pedagogical dynamics by interrogating the relationship between authorship and labor via the means of production in the context of student-authors' work-life balances—which inevitably exist, whether the student is eighteen or forty-eight. To try reassuring student-authors, I repeat that our scheduling/deadlines are flexible and that of course there should be space for "the unexpected." But I also wonder what might be uncovered by following "unexpected" paths more deliberately, rather than merely questioning whether it's something I "should" or "shouldn't" do in my pedagogies. How possible might it also be to break away from what are noted here as masculinist notions of "discipline" and "rigor" in CW practices—which in no way must ever lead to a "perfect draft" but should instead lead to conversations about where drafts are/where they can go, between and among CW peers in the classroom?[27]

GSIs might finally borrow from Abriana Jetté's "Making Meaning: Authority, Authorship, and the Introduction to Creative Writing Syllabus," wherein Jetté examines introductory CW classrooms in the context of authorship and how these contexts get mediated by a CW educator's authority above their student-authors' creativity. As Jetté notes,

> [i]n thinking about the multiple forms of communication and making that students experiment with every day, as well as considering the rhetoric of the pleasure principle, what might students expect to experience when entering a course that describes itself as "wildly inventive?" Will students experiment with mixed media? Listen to music? Use their bodies and their voices as tools of craft? Will there be various opportunities for creative writing students to connect with their peers? With faculty? With established, visiting writers? Perhaps one might expect a syllabus or schedule of assignments that boasts descriptions of "fun" and "pleasure" to deviate from the standard, to remix, to rethink, and/or to reuse language in multiple mediums and ways.[28]

What could it mean for GSIs writing their first-ever CW syllabi to create a "fun" course rather than a labor-heavy one? In other words, how open would GSIs need to be toward the interests of undergraduate student-authors who might wish to compose work in ways that run counter to how the GSI, himself, has learned to practice writing?

This raises questions about student-authors' own writing practices, which include conversations around drafting, revising, and discussing their work in class while trying to discern the "success" of their work in their own eyes, rather than only through the eyes of those who hold explicit power in the classroom (i.e., their instructors).[29] In this endeavor, it can be helpful to focus on methods and materials pointed toward opening fruitful communication between parties—these methods/materials might be effectively utilized among both GSIs and student-authors toward a firmer bridge between differing frames of experience. But first, there needs to be discussion about achieving fruitful communication, on top of how this gets tied to student-authors' aims and the peer assessment/critique around their work.

## Praxis

I'm thinking about a comment from a student-author who wrote in a course evaluation that they "discovered a love of looking inward which I did not even know I had until mid-way through the course," and that "[the instructor] let our voices be our own, merely guiding them to be the best versions possible." Without understanding at the time how successful or unsuccessful my pedagogical aims might've been, I was glad to learn that at least one person felt guided in writing rather than told how to write, and that my approach "let [their] voice be their own" while making room for introspection. I see this as necessary for my own focus in nonfiction pedagogies, which, in a given course, centralize both personal and cultural aspects of creative writing.[30]

A main way my pedagogies have tried to keep student-authors' agency intact has involved their including Authors' Notes with all "high stakes" assignments/ major projects. Guidelines for these are as follows and are adapted from the University of Nebraska-Lincoln Writing Center's "Revision Practices" page:[31]

[a]n *Author's Note* gives your audience the context necessary for them to know how to respond to your writing. In the context of this course, your Author's Note should specifically include the following (and should be about three (3) paragraphs):

Paragraph 1: A statement about the *purpose and audience* of the text, e.g., "This project is an essay communicating my experience with ____ to [X] audience(s)."

Paragraph 2: A sense of the *revision strategies you've already tried*, e.g., "I had my roommate read this project and they suggested changing X, Y, and Z"; "I tried moving paragraphs around, which led to ____"; "I've tried outlining my essay, and I see gaps between my primary and secondary ideas, but I don't know where to go from here."

Paragraph 3: The kind of *response/feedback you're specifically looking for*, e.g., "I'm having trouble understanding how to ____"; "Can you please point to places where my ____ doesn't make sense?";

"The third paragraph on page 2 isn't working for me, but I don't quite know what to do about it . . ." etc.

*The goal*: Author's Notes are the primary way you, as the author, establish the kind of response your writing receives from your audience. Using Author's Notes means knowing ahead of time where you're at with a draft, as well as which kinds of revision plans you might have for the draft. As you become more accustomed to thinking about your drafts in this way, Author's Notes become easier to write, as well as more effective tools for revision, reflection, and response.

Using Author's Notes, student-authors and I together can focus energy/attention on specific parts of their texts. (As in the previous example, if a student-author wants me to pay attention to page 2, then my feedback will focus on page 2.) And since I offer feedback on their major texts/projects in the form of recorded voice notes, whatever I vocally communicate also ends up being a direct response to what they've expressed in their Authors' Notes. This allows trusting they know where they're at in the writing process and attempting to meet them there.

A final way I attempt here to emphasize positioning authorial senses is through revision. Since revision and the "ownership" of a text are so strongly related, revision itself can then benefit student-authors who are in the process of discerning how they actually want their drafts to appear to an audience. This isn't something that happens during a first or early draft but rather throughout the *process* of revision.

GSIs can explore revision practices in their courses to help student-authors navigate authorial senses. Though revision at large is an area of consideration and practice reaching beyond the scope of this chapter, thinking about revision strategies/practices and their effects on student-authors' perceptions of agency can encourage student-authors to articulate the choices they make when moving from one draft to another.[32] Two of the ways I've covered this with student-authors have been through assigning Brenda Miller's "The Shared Space Between Reader and Writer: A Case Study" and Deborah E. Kaplan's "Anne Frank, Reviser." Miller begins by offering drafting and revising processes, also noting that these processes involve using what they've come to call "hermit crab essays"—defined as essays that "adopt already existing forms as the container for the writing at hand, such as the essay in the form of a 'to-do' list, or a field guide, or a recipe."[33]

Miller also notes how they "feel a kind of transformation happening, a new perspective, a moment of forgiveness. It's odd to feel this in one's writing, to feel so concretely that the essay is indeed in charge: speaking to you, telling you things you didn't already know. And this happened solely because of the form."[34] And because the form "doesn't belong to you, it can create meanings— perhaps better meanings—than any you might have thought up on your own"[35] the idea that a form can be "in charge" serves to help student-authors' revision goals. Miller clarifying that the "hermit crab" form encourages them to recognize that this can help bridge gaps between their own intentions and what potential audiences might value about the form(s), what appears in the form(s) itself/themselves, and which forms are commonly valued while certain audiences are kept in mind.

When discussing "We Regret to Inform You," the eventual product of the "hermit crab" processes described earlier (an essay in the form of a rejection letter), Miller explains that

> people are touched by "We Regret to Inform You" not because of the revelation of my personal "rejections," but because I've used a form that invites readers into both my experience and their own. By being ensconced in a more "objective" form, the essay provides what I'll call a "shared space" between reader and writer.[36]

The possibility of a "shared space," a "common ground in the form of an object," should be shared between author and audience. This returns to considering the forms audiences tend to value, pointing student-authors toward considering such value-positions from the perspective of their (target) audience(s).

It has also been helpful to consider revision options with undergraduates through reading Deborah E. Kaplan, who discusses the experience of teaching the definitive edition of Anne Frank's *Diary* to undergraduates who not only have to reconceive the ways they understand Frank as a cultural figure but must also do so through understanding Frank as a dedicated author who completed numerous drafts and regularly practiced revision. In Kaplan's course "Representing the Holocaust," Kaplan and the class together "took a close look at [Frank's] *Diary* edition's foreword in order to track Frank's composing process" as well as Frank's work toward making "already written entries clearer and more vivid, reorder a few of them, and compose new entries for days about which she had not at the time recorded anything."[37] This reveals to student-authors that though Frank is indeed a cultural figure, the *Diary* as an artifact was composed through deliberate textual revision, an acknowledgment that even work in a diary might be made "clearer and more vivid" toward a result desired for target audiences.

One consideration around Kaplan's work is that even diaries can be written (and rewritten) *with* audiences in mind, evidenced by Frank's authorial choices. This may be helpful for student-authors to consider, so that they arrive at a kind of understanding that there isn't outright incompatibility between "honest self-expression" and "audience pleasing."

In fact, bridging the two is a crucial nexus of successful literary nonfiction—especially when authors are familiar with, and can display a respect toward, the audiences for whom they write—such as, for example, with addiction and travel memoirs. As Kaplan discusses learning from teaching Frank's *Diary* in class, student-authors must

> find ways to convey the value of revision for Frank and for writers generally. Creating opportunities for students' own experiences of rewriting while they study the book is one obvious and necessary component, for if students were to attain, through their own experiences of revising, what Joseph Harris (2003: 588) has described as the "sense of an intellectual project," they might be closer to appreciating Frank's discovery of and work on her own. But introducing revision as an explicit topic of discussion, as well as probing beliefs about public and private genres, may also be important when students have little sense of how revising for a general audience can matter to a writer.[38]

Matthew Salesses comments similarly in *Craft in the Real World: Rethinking Fiction Writing and Workshopping* (2021) that if

> it is true that drafts become more and more conscious, more and more based on decisions and less and less on "intuition," then revision is where we can take heart. Revision is the craft through which a writer is able to say and shape who they are and what kind of world they live in. Revision must also be the revision of craft.[39]

This brings to my memory when once, during a day in a course on Kafka while I was an undergraduate, our class talked about artistic processes. Our professor had asked whether we were familiar with what Michelangelo is believed to have said about sculpting processes, to which one classmate raised their hand, then said (trying to paraphrase Michelangelo): "You take a block of marble, and chip everything that isn't the sculpture away." This then became deep-seated as a way for us to revise. (I've also since realized that there are other ways to present revision options that aren't so violently envisioned as that of a chisel.) Revision overall isn't just a matter of "killing your darlings" (another violent image?) but can encompass so many other modes beyond just the previously mentioned "hermit crab" option, for example. In fact, revision can encompass multiple considerations, aligning well not just with a student-author's textual ambitions but also with what they value about how their work becomes presented to the audiences to which they wish to speak.

On top of hermit crab strategies, another way GSIs can encourage student-authors to consider revision strategies beyond the notion of their own line-editing might be through an exercise of "hotspotting" (often more attributed to writing studies than to CW) coupled with reflection on student-authors' own revision practices through the inclusion of an Author's Note.

The University of Nebraska-Lincoln's Writing Center notes that the process of hotspotting involves reflective composing that's "predominately used for revising drafts, but it can also be useful in writing and thinking about other texts you read for class—your peers' and other authors."[40] I give student-authors UNL's steps for hotspotting as follows:

1. Read the draft that you'd like to develop.
2. Reread the draft, marking (underline, highlight, star, etc.) places where you think your writing is working. This could be a sentence that expresses a thought-provoking idea, a strong or startling image, a central tension, or a place that could be explored in more detail. These places are the "hot spots" of your draft.
3. Copy one of the hot spots onto the top of a clean page; then, put your draft aside. (If you are working on a computer, copy the passage and paste it to a new document.) If the passage is long, you can cut it out of the original or fold the draft so only the hot spot shows.
4. Now write, using the hot spot as a new first sentence (or paragraph). Write for fifteen to twenty minutes, or as long as you need to develop your ideas. Don't worry if you'll "lose" your original idea. You might be in the process of finding a better one.

5. Repeat the process as often as feels right. (Shoot for three to four times.)
6. Now put your piece back together. You might want to just add the new writing into the piece or substitute it for something you can now delete. You might even take out large sections of the original writing and reorganize the rest around your new writing. Consider how your conception of the "whole" of this draft changes with the new material.
7. In your Author's Note or writing plan, focus on two things. (1) Write some directions for what you want to do with this writing the next time you work on it. What do you have to change about the text to include the new writing? (2) Reflect upon your revision process. What did you learn about your topic/your text from the process? Did you pursue a tangential idea? Deepen or extend an original idea? Change your perspective on the topic? Realize that you are really interested in another topic altogether?[41]

Since hotspotting is a strategy more common in writing studies courses, for student-authors in CW what I believe I see happening most often with their (hotspotting) process is how often they focus on instances of scene and/or introspection. They'll (especially if composing a narrative) discover that they want the narrative to start in a different place than it initially had; or perhaps they want their work to begin with an idea rather than with the story they first tried telling. This altogether not only helps them solidify agency within/through their texts but also helps discern how successfully they've accomplished their own writing goals as I provide feedback on their work as the instructor while responding to the details they've laid out in Author's Notes.

## Conclusions

I've tried aligning myself with what CW researcher and poet Janelle Adsit articulates in *Toward an Inclusive Creative Writing: Threshold Concepts to Guide the Literary Curriculum* (2017) about CW students and authorship— namely, that student-authors become more fully engaged with writing if they "come to see themselves as writers."[42] This doesn't imply that student-authors need to "adopt the role uncritically or without a complex understanding of what the subject-position is and how it has been constructed," however, not to mention where those constructions come from (or how such constructions enter CW classrooms).[43]

My question for CW is *how* can student-authors "come to see themselves as writers"? Through first insisting that "author" implies agency I also think here about how CW GSIs can examine ways to help student-authors "come to see themselves as writers" while encouraging critical questioning about what authorship means in the context of class communities. According to Adsit, CW student-authors "encounter a range of assumptions about writing reflected in popular culture."[44] It's therefore also

> the responsibility of the creative writing course to help student-writers negotiate these messages, to check these popular constructs against lived experiences, to become better able to critically consider what authorship means for different writers in different times and places. The creative writing class can provide students the opportunity to claim a writerly identity for themselves and to simultaneously critique received cultural ideas about the writerly life.[45]

I hope that in framing authorship in the face of "received cultural ideas" with the (student) authorial identity as one "constructed by cultural forces," GSIs can consider notions of authorship as being helpful for solidifying their positions in CW pedagogies. With many student-authors hoping to become professional/published authors themselves, it feels important for GSIs to have a framework for discussing what the "writing life" may mean (should their student-authors decide to enter it at all) as well as ways GSIs may themselves perpetuate ideas about a "writer's life" with student-authors should they remain instructors in North American higher education writing spaces.

Finally, in my own position as an educator, an author, and a researcher in US university settings, I want to reassess not just the kind of positioning I try taking on as I engage inclusive pedagogies, but also the kinds of pedagogies my student-authors might perceive from their ends. Since my personal trajectory has been threaded throughout higher education in the United States, I'm also interested in interrogating what I've been encouraged to teach by way of the cultural lenses I've operated within (and without).[46]

Positioning might be easy to discuss for CW in North America because it aligns with the discipline's own academic traditions, in that student-authors are often placed in writing scenarios where they're expected to learn from educators' lived experience(s) *as* professional authors. They watch, and they learn. And they're expected to learn from how an educator's résumé does or doesn't influence classroom discussions, or the pedagogies educators enact. The premise is that student-authors are supposed to get something from their educators' experiences, especially if the educator is viewed as a "star."[47] But, star status or not, with student-authors being expected to view CW educators as accomplished while also being encouraged to absorb what they can't gather from authors with less shimmering résumés, this distracts from more wide-angle framing on what student-authors may actually witness in CW pedagogies.

What if what student-authors see turns out to be not what they wished for, though? How can CW in North American higher education go about creating, through more inclusive pedagogies, environments in which student-authors and GSIs alike can thrive?

# Writing Prompts

1. Draft an "origin story" for your pseudonym. Though not required, you might research the etymology of the pseudonym. Overall, disclose why this is "the name of your writer voice."
2. Reflect on realizing you wanted to "become a writer." Consider the following questions: *Did my influences look like me? Which writing rituals—if any—did I borrow from particular persons/environments? If I know (an)other language(s), did I consider only writing in English?*
3. Title your draft "Advice for Writers." In your draft, actively avoid these three phrases: "Find your voice," "Show, don't tell," and "Write what you know."
4. Choose a draft composed earlier in the course. Revise it toward a different form, for example, revising a narrative into a shopping list, rewriting an essay as an email, and turning a memoir excerpt into a press release.

# Notes

1 Haider, Adil. "The Provider Awareness and Cultural Dexterity Toolkit for Surgeons Trial—Full Text View." *U.S. National Library of Medicine*, Brigham and Women's Hospital, July 3, 2018, https://clinicaltrials.gov/ct2/show/NCT03576495.

2   Walker, Alice. *In Search of Our Mothers' Gardens: Womanist Prose*. Open Road Media, 2011.

3   Ibid., p. 12.

4   Ibid., p. 8.

5   To illustrate further: "I'm writing for black [*sic*] people, [Morrison] says, 'in the same way that Tolstoy was not writing for me, a 14-year-old coloured girl from Lorain, Ohio. I don't have to apologise or consider myself limited because I don't [write about white people]—which is not absolutely true, there are lots of white people in my books. The point is not having the white critic sit on your shoulder and approve it.'"

6   Walker, p. 8.

7   hooks, bell. "to gloria, who is she: on using a pseudonym." *Talking Back: Thinking Feminist, Thinking Black*. South End Press, 1989.

8   Ibid., p. 160.

9   Ibid., p. 162.

10   Ibid., p. 163.

11   I try to identify with this regarding any instance of my own work in print in which I see the name Micah McCrary. I recognize, when I'm holding in hand my first book (*Island in the City*) or a print issue of a journal that contains my work that what's presented through those pages is tangibly distinguished (at least for myself) from the person who has lunch with a friend, who's on a video call with his partner, or who travels to visit his family. In a sense, it helps the work to stay the work, placing less pressure onto an assumption that the work is *also* somehow my entire self (when it isn't).

12   hooks, p. 166.

13   Chavez, Felicia Rose. *The Anti-Racist Writing Workshop: How to Decolonize the Creative Classroom*. Haymarket Books, 2021, p. 98.

14   Huber, Sonya. "The Three Words That Almost Ruined Me as a Writer: 'Show, Don't Tell.'" *Literary Hub*, October 7, 2019, https://lithub.com/the-three-words -that-almost-ruined-me-as-a-writer-show-dont-tell/.

15   Ibid.

16   Coleman, Taiyon J. "The Thenar Space: Writing Beyond Emotion and Experience into Story." *How Dare We! Write: A Multicultural Creative Writing Discourse*, 2nd ed., edited by Sherry Quan Lee, Modern History Press, 2022, pp. 110–19. ISBN 978-1-61599-683-4.

17   A similar discussion can be seen in Rachel Blau DuPlessis's *The Pink Guitar: Writing as Feminist Practice* (1990) where DuPlessis writes that an author who is a woman is a "marked marker," and that for a "woman writer" as a cultural

producer the question becomes "how to imagine herself, and how to imagine women, gender, sexualities, men and her own interest when the world of images and, indeed, basic structures of thought have been filled to overflowing with representations of her, and displacements of any 'her' by the representations of others make" (DuPlessis, p. 161). DuPlessis thereby forces the identity of the author onto affirmations of the body, noting that the author who is a woman is also a "woman writer," someone who has become authorized via gender first and then, only after, through writing prowess.

18  Coleman, p. 115.

19  Ibid., p. 114.

20  Hennessy, Rachel. "Am I No Longer a Writer? 'Universal' Tenets and the Writing/ Teaching Self." *New Writing: The International Journal for the Practice and Theory of Creative Writing*, vol. 18, no. 2, 2021, pp. 125–33. doi:10.1080/14790726.2020.1 758153.

21  Ibid., p. 126.

22  Ibid.

23  Clark, Romy, and Roz Ivanič. *The Politics of Writing*. Routledge, 1997.

24  In *Bootstraps: From an American Academic of Color*, Victor Villanueva notes that "[a]s the conscious use of language, rhetoric would include everything that is conveyed through language: philosophy, history, anthropology, psychology, sociology, literature, politics" (Villanueva, p. 117).

25  Hennessy, p. 132.

26  Ibid.

27  GSIs can also refer to "Shitty First Drafts" in Lamott, Anne. *Bird by Bird: Some Instructions on Writing and Life*. Anchor Books, 1997.

28  Jetté, Abriana. "Making Meaning: Authority, Authorship, and the Introduction to Creative Writing Syllabus." *Assay: A Journal of Nonfiction Studies*, vol. 6, no. 1, fall 2019, https://www.assayjournal.com/abriana-jetteacute-making-meaning -authority-authorship-and-the-introduction-to-creative-writing-syllabus-61 .html.

29  Also see: Elbow, Peter. "Writing for Teachers." *Writing with Power: Techniques for Mastering the Writing Process*. Oxford: Oxford University Press, 1998, pp. 216–36.

30  This might also be where an antipatriarchal approach to pedagogies could come in. That is, it's not lost on me that I present as both a man and as nonwhite at the head of a classroom filled by those who are often white-presenting adolescents.

31  More on Author's Notes from UNL's Writing Center here: https://www.unl.edu/ writing/revision-practices#authorsnote.

32	Another resource for GSIs exploring this might include "I Get to Choose What I Want to be Done with My Paper': Teacher Revision Pedagogy, Student Revising Practices, and Student Agency," where Megan L. Titus notes that though much that's written about revision "focuses on *how* to teach revision effectively (such as through peer review) it "doesn't emphasize teaching students how to value that practice, or how to use revision in other ways, such as to forward their agency as writers" (Titus, p. 3). GSIs teaching student-authors about the *value* of revision might steer them toward greater overall comfort with their drafts, as gained through successive revision(s).

33	Miller, Brenda. "The Shared Space Between Reader and Writer: A Case Study." *Brevity: A Journal of Concise Literary Nonfiction*, January 7, 2015, https:// brevitymag.com/craft-essays/the-shared/space/.

34	Ibid.

35	Ibid.

36	Ibid.

37	Kaplan, Deborah E. "Anne Frank, Reviser." *Pedagogy*, vol. 18, no. 1, January 2018, pp. 87–107.

38	Ibid., pp. 100–1.

39	Salesses, Matthew. *Craft in the Real World: Rethinking Fiction Writing and Workshopping.* Catapult, 2021.

40	"Revision Practices." *Writing Center | University of Nebraska-Lincoln*, https://www .unl.edu/writing/revision-practices.

41	"Revision Practices." *Writing Center | University of Nebraska-Lincoln.*

42	Adsit, Janelle. *Toward an Inclusive Creative Writing: Threshold Concepts to Guide the Literary Curriculum.* Bloomsbury Academic, an Imprint of Bloomsbury Publishing Plc, 2017.

43	Ibid., p. 91.

44	Ibid.

45	Ibid.

46	Put another way, if compositionist-poet Patrick Bizzaro's assertions in *Responding to Student Poems: Applications of Critical Theory* (1993) that we "need to remember that how we teach is what we teach" (Bizzaro, p. 10) are en pointe, then what have I "passed on" to student-authors through my pedagogies (and ideologies)? Or, even in my attempts to be conscious of my position in the class community?

47	See Ritter, Kelly. "Ethos Interrupted: Diffusing 'Star' Pedagogy in Creative Writing Programs." *College English*, vol. 69, no. 3, 2007, pp. 283–92. JSTOR, www .jstor.org/stable/25472210.

# Further Reading

Allen, Sarah. "The Inspired Writer vs. The Real Writer." *Writing Spaces: Readings on Writing*, edited by Charles Lowe and Pavel Zemliansky, vol. 1, Parlor Press, 2010, pp. 34–44, https://www.writingspaces.org/volume1.

Baldwin, James. *Notes of a Native Son*. Beacon Press, 2012.

Barthes, Roland. "The Death of the Author." *Aspen*, translated by Richard Howard, 5–6, 1967, www.ubu.com/aspen/aspen5and6/threeEssays.html#barthes.

Bishop, Wendy. "Contracts, Radical Revision, Portfolios, and the Risks of Writing." *Power and Identity in the Creative Writing Classroom: The Authority Project*, edited by Anna Leahy, Multilingual Matters, 2005, pp. 109–20.

Bizzaro, Patrick. *Responding to Student Poems: Applications of Critical Theory*. National Council of Teachers of English, 1993.

Bizzaro, Patrick and Michael McClanahan. "Putting Wings on the Invisible: Voice, Authorship, and the Authentic Self." *Can It Really Be Taught? Resisting Lore in Creative Writing Pedagogy*, edited by Kelly Ritter and Stephanie Vanderslice, Boynton/Cook Heinemann, 2007, pp. 77–90.

Brady, Tess. "Interrogating Authorships: Students Writing Hypertext." *TEXT: Journal of Writing and Writing Courses*, vol. 3, no. 2, October 1999, www.textjournal.com.au/oct99/brady.htm.

Brooke, Robert. "Modeling a Writer's Identity: Reading and Imitation in the Writing Classroom." *College Composition and Communication*, vol. 39, no. 1, 1998, pp. 23–41. JSTOR, www.jstor.org/stable/357814.

DuPlessis, Rachel Blau. *The Pink Guitar: Writing as Feminist Practice*. Routledge, 1990.

Forbes, Elizabeth. "Multiple Facets of the Developing Writer." *New Writing: The International Journal for the Practice and Theory of Creative Writing*, vol. 14, no. 2, 2017, pp. 265–74, https://doi.org/10.1080/14790726.2020.1758153.

Foucault, Michel. "What Is an Author?" *Language, Counter-Memory, Practice: Selected Essays and Interviews by Michel Foucault*, edited by Donald F. Bouchard, translated by Donald F. Bouchard and Sherry Simon, Cornell University Press, 1977, pp. 113–38.

Glover, Stuart. "Creative Writing Studies, Authorship, and the Ghosts of Romanticism." *New Writing: The International Journal for the Practice and Theory of Creative Writing*, vol. 9, no. 3, 2012, pp. 293–301, https://doi.org/10.1080/14790726.2012.693097.

Greene, Stewart. "Making Sense of My Own Ideas: The Problems of Authorship in a Beginning Writing Classroom." *Written Communication*, vol. 12, no. 2, April 1995, pp. 186–218, https://doi.org/10.1177/0741088395012002002.

Harris, Joseph. "Revision as a Critical Practice." *College English*, vol. 65, no. 6, 2003, pp. 577–92.

Hennessy, Rachel. "Am I No Longer a Writer? 'Universal' Tenets and the Writing/ Teaching Self." *New Writing: The International Journal for the Practice and Theory of Creative Writing*, vol. 18, no. 2, pp. 125–33, 2021. https://Doi.org/10.1080 /14790726.2020.1758153.

Hoby, Hermione. "Toni Morrison: 'I'm Writing for Black People . . . I Don't Have to Apologise.'" *The Guardian*, Guardian News and Media, April 25, 2015, https:// theguardian.com/books/2015/apr/25/toni-morrison-books-interview-god-help -the-child.

Horner, Bruce. "Students, Authorship, and the Work of Composition." *College English*, vol. 59, no. 5, 1997, pp. 505–29. JSTOR, www.jstor.org/stable/ 378664.

Ivanič, Roz. *Writing and Identity: The Discoursal Construction of Identity in Academic Writing*. John Benjamins, 1998.

Jetté, Abriana. "Making Meaning: Authority, Authorship, and the Introduction to Creative Writing Syllabus." *Assay: A Journal of Nonfiction Studies*, vol. 6, no. 1, fall 2019, https://www.assayjournal.com/abriana-jetteacute-making-meaning -authority-authorship-and-the-introduction-to-creative-writing-syllabus-61 .html.

Morales Kearns, Rosalie. "Voice of Authority: Theorizing Creative Writing Pedagogy." *College Composition and Communication*, vol. 60, no. 4, 2009, pp. 790–807. JSTOR, www.jstor.org/stable/40583430.

Petty, Audrey. "Who's The Teacher? From Student to Mentor." *Power and Identity in the Creative Writing Classroom: The Authority Project*, edited by Anna Leahy, Multilingual Matters, 2005, pp. 77–86.

Ritchie, Joy S. "Beginning Writers: Diverse Voices and Individual Identity." *College Composition and Communication*, vol. 40, no. 2, 1989, pp. 152–74.

Ritter, Kelly. "Professional Writers/Writing Professionals: Revamping Teacher Training in Creative Writing Ph.D. Programs." *College English*, vol. 64, no. 2, 2001, pp. 205–27. JSTOR, www.jstor.org/stable/1350117.

Silko, Leslie Marmon. *Yellow Woman and a Beauty of the Spirit: Essays on Native American Life Today*. Simon & Schuster, 1997.

St. Amant, Kirk. "Writing in Global Contexts: Composing Usable Texts for Audiences from Different Cultures." *Writing Spaces: Readings on Writing*, edited by Dana Driscoll, Mary Stewart, and Matthew Vetter, vol. 3, Parlor Press, 2020, pp. 147–61, writingspaces.org/node/1708.

Titus, Megan L. "'I Get to Choose What I Want to Be Done with My Paper': Teacher Revision Pedagogy, Student Revising Practices, and Student Agency." *Journal of*

*Teaching Writing*, vol. 32, January 2018, pp. 1–31, https://journals.iupui.edu/index
.php/teachingwriting/article/view/22279.

Villanueva, Victor. *Bootstraps: From an American Academic of Color.* National
Council of Teachers of English, 1993.

Walker, Alice. *In Search of Our Mothers' Gardens: Womanist Prose.* Betascript
Publishing, 1983.

3

# Why Bother in English? On Creative Writing's Translingual Potential

One thing creative writing (CW) pedagogies may not have reckoned with quite yet with full potential is that of English monolingualism in the classroom. Writing studies scholars have, by contrast, long acknowledged "English-only" policies, and they've carried work beyond those policies to recognize aspects of writing instruction that connect to a monolingual hierarchy. These tensions have allowed (undergraduate) student-authors access to language use within their own writing practices, maybe even as part of a movement toward translingual class communities.[1]

The existence of two programs at the University of Iowa—for instance, its MFA in Spanish Creative Writing and the MFA in Literary Translation—might evidence how CW's own institutional relationship to plurilingual student-authors has started gaining acceptance in North American higher education. MFA programs in translation are currently less widespread than their CW counterparts, though such programs continue cropping up not just in places like Iowa but also at NYU, in the University of Texas El Paso's Bilingual Creative Writing program, the MFA in Creative Writing for Writers of Spanish at Hofstra University (New York), in the University of Arkansas Fayetteville—Program in Creative Writing and Translation; and some others.[2]

Together, GSIs and student-authors can observe the growth of programs like these to (1) benefit from addressing a position on language use in CW, (2) delineate language and agency to position the CW classroom as a site of translingual action, and (3) address not just language's artistic aspects in class communities, but also its cultural aspects. To establish for student-authors ways they might utilize their translanguaging statuses and selves, this could involve establishing CW *as* a translingual site from the onset. This chapter therefore outlines how a cultural dexterity framework attempts a focus on student-authors from various language backgrounds—especially in the goal to examine how, for instance, writing studies has long battled English-only policies. It's CW's turn now.

This works toward ways translingual models for nonfiction may nudge GSIs closer to recognizing and incorporating language diversity—rather than treating the classroom space as only (English) monolingual and additionally highlighting the increased number of international and nonnative English student-authors in CW classrooms throughout recent years. And, as Module 2 for the proposed PACTS curriculum is expressed as "communicating effectively with patients with limited English proficiency," a similar aim can be expressed through a culturally dexterous CW outcome like the following: *In this course, student-authors will prepare to collaborate with peers from diverse language traditions and backgrounds.*[3]

# (Classroom) Acts of Reclamation

I care about imagining this outcome because I've long been interested in languages and in language justice and equity. I studied three non-English languages while going through school—four semesters of Spanish during high school, three semesters of Japanese as an undergraduate, and five semesters of French spread throughout undergraduate and graduate study. (I wanted to study German in junior high, but my parents made it clear no one in the family could help me.) I'll cover French here because I've stuck with it the longest—not just through formal classroom experience but also in practical use throughout some of my travel outside the United States. But to situate things a bit, I want to connect my feelings/perceptions around French to first telling you about Félicité.

The story I was told: Félicité (who also went by Felicity and Filise) was a Chahta girl who once lived on her tribal nation's reservation in what we now recognize as Louisiana. At some point during childhood, an aunt came and took her off the reservation and then placed her in a school run by Acadian missionaries. Through this schooling, Filise's first language (Chahta Anumpa) was lost and replaced with Parisian French; she eventually picked up some English, too. Filise grew up to meet a man through local trading named Lucien, who was biracial of Black and Acadian descent. Through this union, Filise and Lucien became my maternal great-great-grandparents.

Even though it makes me jealous, I like hearing and learning about Filise through phone conversations with my maternal grandmother's cousin, Dan (b. 1938), who was partly raised by Filise and who, through his luck, got to experience living in a plurilingual (French, Louisiana Creole, and English) home on top of learning about any Native traditions (mostly through food) Filise was able to pass down while keeping language traditions alive. Dan tells me Filise's English was weak, that Parisian French was her strength, and that her world outside the home was primarily Louisiana Creole and Anglophone. Through everything I learn about Filise, I feel an even stronger gravity toward French—not because of its status as a European Romance language but because it's part of my heritage, keeping both Filise and Lucien in mind as I practice.

I recognize the complications here of French being simultaneously a colonizing language and the closest thing my family may have to a heritage language, but even with these complications I try to learn, practice, and study, whether in formal spaces or not. I spent five summers (totaling over a year of my life) in France; I've tried as often as possible in my adulthood to visit places like Genève and more recently Montréal; and I consume much French media— including watching Francophone TV/film, learning music lyrics, and reading "bandes dessinées" (comics/graphic novels) to help me practice. I suppose that, in my resolve to keep working through all this, I recognize my practicing French not merely as an act of study but also as an act of reclamation.

## Breaking (out of) English: The Languages of Our Souls

I hope to help student-authors in my courses reclaim their agency with language(s), too, and one way I've attempted getting them to consider the proximity between their identities and their language use in class communities has been through reading with them bell hooks's "Language: Teaching New Worlds/New Words." This chapter from *Teaching to Transgress: Education as the Practice of Freedom* (1994) uses as part of its foundation Adrienne Rich's poem "The Burning of Paper Instead of Children," wherein Rich has written the line, "[t]his is the oppressor's language yet I need it to talk to you."[4] hooks is pulled to think about the line somewhat incessantly—not just around her own language practices but also the language practices in which she asks her student-authors to consider and partake. For instance, hooks writes about Rich's poem that

> when I first read these words, and now, they make me think of standard English, of learning to speak against black [sic] vernacular, against the ruptured and broken speech of a dispossessed and displaced people. Standard English is not the speech of exile. It is the language of conquest and domination; in the United States, it is the mask which hides the loss of so many tongues, all those sounds of diverse, native communities we will never hear, the speech of the Gullah, Yiddish, and so many unremembered tongues.[5]

When I see "unremembered tongues" I think about any of the languages lost through the progression of my own Black, First American, and European lineage. But I also remember here one Chinese student-author (in an academic writing rather than a CW course) who once said during class that "Learning English feels like learning a second language, but learning academic English feels like learning a third language." This influenced me to alter my pedagogies dramatically in writing studies and CW courses alike—considering how various Englishes can bear different weights onto different student-authors, especially when they're learning to enter writing situations in ways that can feel inauthentic to themselves and to their own language practices.[6] And when I'm brought to think about how "[s]tandard English is not the speech of exile" but rather "the language of conquest and domination" I consider our English language use in North American class communities more widely, on top of how we're encouraged to think these uses should be inflexible—subtracting any possibility around what we're now able to recognize as translingual practices and discourses.

In "Language," hooks also recounts an experience of asking

> an ethnically diverse group of students in a course I was teaching on black [sic] women writers why we only heard standard English spoken in the classroom, they were momentarily rendered speechless. Though many of them were individuals for whom standard English was a second or third language, it had simply never occurred to them that it was possible to say something in another language, in another way.[7]

Something similar often shows up in the conversations I have with nonnative English student-authors for whom it has perhaps never occurred to use "untranslatable" words in their L1 (first language) in their texts. In my current geography this usually appears in the form of student-authors from Latine and Chinese ethnic backgrounds who hold a keen sense of a meaning of a word existing in Spanish/ Mandarin/Cantonese but not in English—when I tell them just to write the word in their L1, a common reaction is a wide-eyed "I can do that!?" This offers opportunity to more commonly consider the options given to student-authors working from diverse language backgrounds, getting us to think as educators about how we can attend to these backgrounds in the pedagogies we design and enact.

hooks finally notes that

> it is evident that we must change conventional ways of thinking about language, creating spaces where diverse voices can speak in words other than English or in broken, vernacular speech. This means that at a lecture or even in a written work there will be fragments of speech that may or may not be accessible to every individual. Shifting how we think about language and how we use it necessarily alters how we know what we know.[8]

The act of "shifting how we think about language and how we use it" and changing "conventional ways of thinking about language" will offer opportunities in class communities to allow all student-authors, regardless of language background, to consider how they might access their most native language resources in their writing—even those for whom Standard American English (SAE) is their dominant or only language.[9] One effect this could have is a plurilingual class community not only allowing but encouraging all student-authors to reconceptualize (and perhaps, in the process, decolonialize) their thought and action around English language use more widely.

I've long been in love with exemplifying these "shifts" through also giving student-authors Marlina Gonzalez's "Dancing between Bamboos or The Rules of Wrong Grammar." This is because Gonzalez grapples with the idea of being "a multilingual writer by historical default" within the geography of the Philippines, where so much language use has remained institutionalized and politicized rather than passed down through heritage. As a result, being "a multilingual writer by historical default" puts Gonzalez in a position to discern how to mediate language use not just in daily life but also in writing-related decision-making.

Gonzalez's essay opens with the line, "[m]y challenge as one who speaks and writes in more than one tongue is having the puzzlement of a two-laned writing brain."[10] I imagine this as a relatable point for plurilingual student-authors who need to choose between which rhetorics and diction to use based on their own language resources. The notion of a "two-laned writing brain" also suggests a need to more commonly examine situations where language choice isn't a matter of being either monolingual or plurilingual but, rather, a matter of observing the diverse language traditions that flow through student-authors' writing.

This observation can come through Gonzalez illustrating that

> [w]illful multilingual writers make a conscious choice to write in one of their chosen languages. Being a multilingual writer by historical default, my conscious and unconscious languages flow into and battle each other, with one language (English) wanting to dominate the narrative while the language of my heritage (Tagalog) insists on asserting its irresistible eloquence. But together, Taglish or Engalog is/are the language/s of my soul. One cannot exist without the other.[11]

I love carrying this into questions: How might it look to ask student-authors to compose in "the languages of their souls"? Would or could this result in more common translanguaging practices in class communities?[12] (How) would this affect the ways student-authors discuss their work in peer review/workshop? Might it open doors to broader creativity on the part of student-authors expanding their repertoires by way of their language use, rather than merely their imagination?

Gonzalez finally notes that like many student-authors (I imagine) they "have always written bilingually" but asks, "how does one do that in a culture that insists on erasing my bilinguality, which, by the way, is the result of expeditions and conquests by the very same culture?"[13] This seems akin to the ways writing studies educators have already tried resisting English-only policies—a next step must then involve what this resistance can look like through the conversations about pedagogy and language happening in CW class communities.[14]

## Breaking (out of) English: Meaning-Making, Literature, and Deafness

As another way to engage diverse language traditions in CW, I often take an opportunity to cover American Sign Language (ASL) and Deafness as part of these traditions with student-authors. That is, the language traditions we cover in class communities don't only need to encompass only those spoken and heard: we can also capitalize on visual (and other) modes of communicating that help frame the thinking that takes place in the class community. In particular, through Kristen Harmon's "Writing Deaf: Textualizing Deaf Literature" student-authors often report opening up to ASL in translingual contexts, being brought to consider Deaf authors as needing to switch codes in order to write for Anglophone audiences—rather than those for whom ASL is their primary language resource.[15] Harmon notes that

> [i]f fiction writers or poets happen to be Deaf—meaning that they consider themselves to be members of the Deaf community and use ASL as their primary language—then they must also consider how writing in English (or other print languages) displaces a cultural identity grounded in a visual-spatial language, one that has historically been denigrated, suppressed, and erased from sight.[16]

This allows an opportunity to consider language marginalization further, especially when student-authors have already considered this marginalization through discussing English-only policies (and even outright language prejudice). It's helpful to consider these contexts when student-authors are asked to think about how ASL has "been denigrated, suppressed, and erased from sight," offering an angle through which to investigate ASL in these very contexts.

Harmon notes it's "important to remember that many Deaf people who are creative writers and who are innovative in their use of ASL simply do not bother with writing literary forms of English" and "for the purposes of writing Deaf, why bother with English? It is, after all, the dreaded and always fragmented, incomplete language of speech therapy: words forced, unwieldy and thick, from mouths."[17] I love the question "Why bother with English?"; of course, it's expressed here in the contexts of Deaf/Hard of Hearing (HoH) authors, but in many circumstances could be broadened toward authors for whom English isn't a primary language resource.[18] Especially when we consider creative writing acts themselves, and what language innovation in CW might entail, applying a Deaf lens to the issue can help the class community process how language gets played with and remains malleable toward student-authors' creative output.

This connects to a final idea student-authors can borrow from Harmon, being that

> [b]y pointing out the slipperiness of meaning, by breaking English, by making over English into hybrid forms, and by demanding that the reader *look*, Deaf writers are slowly raising a resistant, disruptive, subaltern presence with a gathering collective locus of agency. By commandeering written English and insisting upon our status as a bilingual, bicultural people living in a diglossic subculture, Deaf writers theorize a relationship with a dominating language. It does not valorize or covet agency made available in that language but instead begins to break it apart on the page, begins to see even the word, the layout on the page, as a mode of resistance.[19]

I wish for student-authors marginalized through language to see their own resources not just as "modes of resistance" but also for them to "theorize a relationship with a dominating language." Similar to how Marlina Gonzalez works through personal relationships to Tagalog, Spanish, and English, I hope Harmon's work offers student-authors even more impetus toward their senses of language agency by way of witnessing Deaf meaning-making as an example of resistance. Especially through Harmon, who offers examples of how ASL poetry can look when transliterated, student-authors from diverse language backgrounds can use these examples to imagine how their own translanguaging practices might not just bolster their agency but also broaden their creative output.

## Breaking (out of) English: Workshopping China

Though I don't typically discuss "international" workshop contexts with student-authors in US settings, I do think about the potential for non-US models to influence my pedagogies. In particular, one resource I've kept in mind has been "Creative Writing as Education in the Chinese Context," where educator Fan Dai illustrates benefits to student-authors in a program implemented at Sun Yet-sen University—piggybacking on CW practices and pedagogies that emerged in Chinese higher (or "tertiary") education in 2006 at Fudan University and Renmin University, both in China. Fudan's program is conducted both in Chinese and in English, the Renmin program is solely in English, and the course Dai set up at Sun Yet-sen was established for student-authors to use autobiographical nonfiction in English "so that students, as new writers, can turn to their own lives for inspiration."[20] And since there hasn't "been a tradition of teaching creative writing at the university level, research regarding creative writing in China has so far focused on introducing the components and teaching methods used in the West and on the recognition of creative writing as an academic discipline."[21] Though there isn't an established CW model in China there does seem to be a model in development—taken from the (Western) normative workshop but expressed through a Chinese context (and therefore, slightly changing how the model can operate). Dai doesn't mention the workshop's "gag rule," for example, and her nonfiction class is set up in other ways that don't exactly *resemble* the normative workshop.

Dai's structure shows how student-authors are introduced to CW while gaining practices in English composing, particularly in a creative rather than an academic context:

> I combine the Western workshop model with my experiences of teaching English as a second or foreign language, but make adjustments according to how a particular group of students respond to the teaching. The pedagogical framework I have developed since 2009 includes the following components: reading as a writer, workshops, peer correction/appreciation, teacher assessment (which includes comments and grading), revisions, summary lectures on each assignment, a creative project called "Going Beyond the Boundary" and a final creative performance. Neither of the last two is graded.[22]

Not only is this nonnormative in presentation, but Dai's more "traditional" components that feel usable here are (1) workshops positioned toward "peer correction/appreciation" and (2) summary lectures—though "correction" would need to be further defined for North American student-author demographics.

Toward implementing the workshops for Chinese student-authors as ELLs, Dai mentions two primary functions the workshop provides, which involve

> enhancing students' critical thinking and providing them with a platform to understand more about each other. Students enjoy the role of constructive reader, which they do not play otherwise, and they appreciate the opportunity to critique classmates' work and get to know them better. As Feng [a student] described it, "during the workshop we can share our experiences associated

with the two essays with the whole class. We can share, discuss, debate . . .
which makes me feel we are the masters of our own classes."[23]

It's worth noting that Dai uses nonfiction texts like Joan Didion's "In Bed" and
Brian Doyle's "Being Brians" to teach aspects of "plain" US life and culture.
Readings like these might help encourage student-authors to become "aware of
cultural differences, an important aspect of writing for international readers."[24]
Didion's essay revolves around accepting that migraines are an unavoidable
part of her life, and Doyle covers the seemingly trite subject of names and
identity, both of which can help Chinese student-authors understand how
literary essays are used to investigate the culturally quotidian.

This makes it possible to imagine a similar framework for student-authors
in US institutions. Dai's conversations with student-authors about "plain
American life" can point to many nonfiction texts that might be used in US
workshops—meant to give student-authors awareness of "plain" life in cultures
that aren't their own, especially when what's considered everyday in other
cultures may be misaligned with their own understandings of what's normal or
routine. It could also subtract any impetus for international student-authors to
feel they need to have lived "amazing" lives in order to then write about them.

That the course at Sun Yat-sen focuses on nonfiction also seems to be a
helpful and smart way to introduce student-authors to CW. If they lack a sense
of invention/creativity because they haven't been exposed to CW as a practice,
starting with autobiography can help nonnative English student-authors
generate material because of how they're already able to reflect on their lives.
This is similar to introductory courses in US composition programs (which
often involve assignments like literacy narratives, personal essays, and other
types of "life writing") where student-authors can use nonfiction to reflect
on experiences they have strong memories of or reactions to. And, just as in
writing studies, CW educators wouldn't necessarily need to require that most
"elementary" student-authors begin autobiographically. If a goal is to introduce
them to CW as a practice, then studying other authors' lives alongside
exploring their senses of self can help their authorial self-perceptions develop
and mature.

There's finally a context of agency here to tie to workshopping in China:
Dai's student-authors sense an authority in CW that isn't received from their
other curricula and that helps them *enjoy* CW, while nudging them toward

becoming "the masters of their own classes." In a way, they've taken charge of their own education, and GSIs can locate avenues toward this for helping nonnative English student-authors feel like "masters" of their language(s) in CW activity.

## GSI Resources

When it comes to GSIs helping student-authors "master" language resources in the class community, resources abound. Most included here I've taken from writing studies, sociolinguistics, and so on toward a transdisciplinarity that aims to help GSIs think as broadly as possible about the wells they might dip into to help student-authors in their courses.

It can help GSIs to look at Cristina Sánchez-Martín's "Beyond Language Difference in Writing: Investigating Complex and Equitable Practices" as one such resource where the author forwardly supports recognizing language difference in the writing class community as a benefit toward student-authors. Sánchez-Martín offers numerous examples (and potential solutions) to capitalize on language difference toward the benefit of student-authors who access writing from multiple language positions, also addressing myths of monolingualism and standardization in US writing classrooms.

Sánchez-Martín notes that the goal of their essay is to "inquire about the role of language difference in the learning of writing, especially in academic settings where normative and exclusionary views of language and writing dominate."[25] It seems crucial to single out "normative and exclusionary views of language and writing" especially around (language) standardization's pervasiveness, and how this pervasiveness has remained boring at best (and oppressive at worst) for student-authors trying to capitalize on their language resources. This detracts from an ability for student-authors to realize their senses of agency, and instead forces them into rote processes of composing that often present themselves as more uniform than unique.

Addressing myths of monolingualism/standardization could also be one way of accepting language difference in (at least) US writing classrooms: If we begin to dialogue about teaching student-authors to not just use "one single version of English" in writing studies, then the same should be applied in CW, in that this evokes concerns around language (in)justice on the part of educators who do encourage only one kind of language use in their classrooms.[26] In CW, GSIs can encourage student-authors to consider how their own language resources might stretch toward a fuller potential within the boundaries of their creativity and imagination, and toward their efforts to compose the best writing they can.

Sánchez-Martín brings this point home by asserting that

> as writers, we must approach language difference in more complex ways, since arguments about its use are not just linguistic. As a writer, you can consider ways to celebrate and integrate language difference in your writing. For example, when I write different articles, lesson plans, emails, or reports, I make intentional efforts to not limit my language practices on the basis of language myths. However, sometimes I am discouraged from using specific expressions, a direct translation from Spanish, abbreviations, emojis, etc. And when that happens, instead of merely blaming myself for not knowing the "correct" choice, I wonder: how much space for language difference is there in this type of writing? Are the audiences receptive to it? How much have the myths of monolingualism and standard language shaped the audiences' expectations for what is appropriate or not? What would happen if I decide to ignore the audience's preferences?[27]

I'm into these questions since they're appropriate not just for a writing studies context but also for CW. Especially since as student-authors begin the processes of reflecting on their work, they can also begin envisioning audiences' interaction with the work through adhering to or departing from the myths of (English) monolingualism and "standard language" use.

In my own teaching experiences, I've sometimes found myself telling student-authors to alienate me as their reader when they find the need to utilize multiple language resources in their writing. In the context of their work, this sometimes looks like a student-author composing a text presented mostly in English but also using "untranslatable" words/phrases from a dialect/sociolect/idiolect standpoint; in these cases, I tell them not to worry about searching for any English meaning-making.[28] Especially if they do have target audiences in mind, for example, a Latine student-author envisioning a Spanish-speaking target audience, this student-author can perform much of the same work we observe from authors like Julia Alvarez, Gloria Anzaldúa, Sandra Cisneros, and more, in ensuring that English and Spanish operate together in the text. This happens just as well with my Chinese student-authors, Black student-authors, and others—any of who can, with a little encouragement, locate effective ways to insert multiple and various language resources into texts that don't need to meet any expectation of US English standardization.

On a similar note, in "Workin' Languages: Who We Are Matters in Our Writing" by Sara P. Alvarez, Amy J. Wan, and Eunjeong Lee, the authors advocate for their students to weave native language resources with writing toward achieving senses of agency in the texts/media produced in class. The authors attempt directing student-authors toward focusing on language use itself (whether approached from an English L1 background or not) while getting them to centrally consider how and whether they attach their own writing practices to what the authors identify as a "monolingual ideology." To start, Alvarez, Wan, and Lee write that their

> various experiences of learning what writing is, and how we should practice it, unfortunately, have often enforced a *deficit perspective*. When it comes to writing, ideas about what is "appropriate" are often at the heart of judgments about whether writing, and by extension the author, is "good." These judgments also often connect to what social scientists identify as a process of racialization, by which specific and codified racial meanings are applied to communities of people, their languages and cultural practices. Thus, judgments on "good" writing extend inequities and negative racial codings in our society while suppressing our linguistic and cultural pluralism.[29]

The authors' emphasis on how their experiences have (unfortunately, as they note) "enforced a deficit perspective" reinforces what can be identified through linguistics as *subtractive bilingualism*: This ties to ways language becomes instilled throughout education frameworks as pointing toward English as a replacement of an L1 rather than supplementing an L1 (i.e., *additive bilingualism*) and which connects to the experiences of racialized students navigating school systems while acquiring English as a second or foreign language.

To avoid a "deficit perspective" by taking subtractive bilingualism away from the classroom, Alvarez, Wan, and Lee note their belief that

> who we are and how we critically use language matters in our writing is sustained by an understanding of language identified as *translingualism*. An approach that resists monolingual ideology, translingualism views our

different and varied language practices as critical in inquiring, supporting, and sustaining the full range of richness in our voices. [. . .] While translingualism as pedagogy should be taken up collectively—by schools and committed educators who are judging and assessing your writing—many of your writing practices can also reflect this *translingual orientation.* [30]

To join this "collective," it could be helpful for CW GSIs to envision how a "translingual orientation" might look. I've already mentioned encouraging student-authors to compose using their most native language resources when and where they can, but CW educators might also explore options for how monolingual English student-authors can do so while enacting agency (i.e., authorship) in their work via creativity with language itself. Through strategies like the ones Alvarez, Wan, and Lee provide, this can encourage student-authors from monolingual and plurilingual backgrounds alike to recognize the ways they're *already* translanguaging, which might involve pointing toward practices of code-switching and code-meshing on top of ways student-authors become accustomed to performing multimodal (commented on more fully later) writing and communication.

Alvarez, Wan, and Lee finally note that

[w]riting for our communities can also come down to how we do language in our writing to better reach our communities. This can mean that we might have to go beyond what's conventionally understood as an "essay," or even "writing." For instance, what languages should we use to make our writing most understood by our audience? Is our alphabetic writing the most impactful choice? Should we include images, sound, and colors? How can we best explain an idea? With whose words, stories, experiences, and examples, and in what language(s)? [31]

These questions seem to provide an advocacy for imagining translingual CW class communities. If questions like these get approached head-on, especially alongside student-authors' own explorations of the kinds of projects/assignments they might be able to compose in class, it could lead to even more examples of not just translingual writing products themselves but also products that play off notions of both linguistic and modal accessibility.

* * *

It's also important for CW GSIs to discern their student-authors' own language needs, which can involve focusing on any Englishes student-authors might encounter through the literature GSIs assign to their class communities. This could be illustrated simultaneously through translanguaging and border pedagogy—for example, with a Black student-author accustomed to African American Language (AAL) seeing how their language use comes to life on the page through witnessing other authors (e.g., Toni Morrison, Zora Neale Hurston, and Alice Walker) doing the same.[32]

This can be addressed first by discussing how border pedagogy can lead to concrete translanguaging efforts in CW class communities, and GSIs might navigate this through Tricia Brady's "Negotiating Linguistic Borderlands, Valuing Linguistic Diversity, and Incorporating Border Pedagogy in a College Composition Classroom." The benefit here can be through Brady's observation that border pedagogy (coined by educational theorist Henry Giroux) itself

> focuses on the need for valuing linguistic diversity at institutions of American higher education by discussing what happened when I brought "border pedagogy" (Giroux 28) into a unit of my English 101 course to disrupt the traditional monolingual approach to teaching English, which often "forces . . . students to erase their language differences . . . in order to enjoy an equal opportunity for success."[33]

Brady attempts to fluidly "disrupt the traditional monolingual approach to teaching English." In doing so, rather than establish a kind of solid "border" in the class community, Brady attempts to show how language can act as a porous border by "forc[ing] students to erase their language differences." Brady wants student-authors to remain aware that movement through/within such a border is possible rather than just operating on the assumptions of North American institutions of higher education—which seem to imply that SAE is a border *so* concrete it can only be crossed through acquiring and becoming proficient in academic language.

I mainly consider how GSIs might give student-authors opportunities to confront, and more thoroughly consider, the pervasiveness of SAE as a "monolingual ideology" while possibly disrupting it *through* student-authors' creative writing by seeing how it has pervaded North American higher education and affects peers with language backgrounds other than student-authors' own. "Mainstream pedagogical writing practices are generally complicit with policies for assimilation into a discourse community that expects proficient use of SAE," as Brady writes. And "[f]or this reason, they do not encourage faculty to recognize students' marginal experiences."[34] Student-authors might already internalize an ideology attached to "proper" English on top of notions that SAE is a "key" to social advancement, upward economic mobility, and more. Especially for student-authors in CW, they can turn this expectation on its head, using it to devise ways to compose texts that show they understand—rhetorically, reflexively, and creatively—what they've done by usurping "standard" English.

\*    \*    \*

Another direction GSIs can take involves holding conversations with student-authors about postcolonial literary translation.[35] And it's through an "effect of the imbalance of power relations between colonized and colonizer" (Nasrullah Mambrol) that offers an opportunity here to consider student-authors' translation choices—not just those made regarding a target text but also the choice(s) made in translating the text in the first place. This helps put student-translators face-to-face with the authors of their source texts—which might require considering translations of the work of queer authors while straight and cis-, of a nonwhite author while white, of a cis woman while a cis man, and so on. This directs educators toward a chance for student-translators to have conversations about *why* they choose the authors they do.

For my own first experiences with literary translation, there were of course authors and texts I was given through course assignments; ultimately, I published some of my translations of French work by Rainer Maria Rilke because I was already familiar with his translated work (in German) and I wanted to engage with it further on my own terms. At the time, this looked like engaging more with his work in French (since I don't read, write, or speak any German) on top of considering ways to increase Rilke's readership (at least of his French work) when so many of his fans commonly gravitate toward his German work. I now try reflecting on this choice not in terms of deciding to bring more attention to the work of an already famous author, but in terms of the fact that I as a nonwhite person translated work by a white author, giving me food for thought around my own exigencies toward translating Rilke (as opposed, for example, to the work of Négritude, Middle Eastern, and other authors who also compose French literature).

In "Postcolonial Translation Theory," a review-essay by Nasrullah Mambrol of *Gender in Translation: Cultural Identity and the Politics of Translation* (1996) by Sherry Simon, *Sitting Translation: History, Poststructuralism, and the Colonial Context* (1992) by Tejaswini Niranjana, and *Post-Colonial Translation: Theory and Practice* (1999) edited by Susan Bassnett and Harish Trivedi, Mambrol notes how "[t]he linking of colonization and translation is accompanied by the argument that translation has played an active role in the colonization process and in disseminating an ideologically motivated image of colonized peoples."[36] This seems to emerge most clearly when talking with (especially white) student-authors about any choices they might make toward translating source texts by nonwhite authors. I've mostly seen this with white student-authors who have experiences with East Asian languages (e.g., Mandarin and Japanese) so it's interesting to read in their Author's Notes/commentaries about how they chose the author(s) they did based on a familiarity with the source language, rather than a consideration of who the authors were as people. I made similar choices around Rilke, in some ways—I was attracted, first, to his French poetry and, second, to the fact that he was already a famous/beloved figure.

With student-authors choosing to translate work not from their own traditions or heritages, this grazes the tip of how translation (really, around notions of translation and power) helps them better consider not just their choices regarding the authors with whom they engage but also helpfully situates them in a position to address the question, "Who am I to translate this work?"

# Praxis

To help situate this all in CW class communities, there need to be options for engaged GSIs to foster translingual nonfiction classrooms. One option to explore can involve having student-authors experiment with graphic and/or multimodal nonfiction.[37]

To cover graphic nonfiction: If "a picture is worth a thousand words," then it may be important to note that conveying experience through a deliberately visual medium might be more impactful for some audiences than trying to communicate experience just through alphanumeric text. Graphic nonfiction can focus on conveying experience(s) in ways that are helpful for audiences with language resources that don't always incorporate SAE.[38] This can involve GSIs reading with student-authors the work of those like Alison Bechdel (*Fun Home: A Family Tragicomic*) or Ellen Forney (*Marbles: Mania, Depression, Michelangelo, and Me*) or Kristen Radtke (*Seek You: A Journey through American Loneliness*) and being willing to convince student-authors that they don't need a famous artist's skills for graphic nonfiction.[39] In other words, this is a medium that can help student-authors relax toward assignments that have them break out of English in their work (helping audiences do so, too).

Another departing territory can involve film and video essays. Many have argued (at least since William Costanzo's "Film as Composition") that the consumption and production of film and video can be a way to reconsider student-authors' composing practices: for a twenty-first-century context, examining film/video essays as CW genres might be of help to student-authors trying to depart from English as a "default." I pull in video essayist John Bresland here as an example toward discussing the potential of film/video in CW. In "On the Origin of the Video Essay" Bresland provides reasoning for CW educators to support video, noting that

> [t]oday artists have access to video editing tools that ship free on most computers. A generation ago, such capability didn't exist at any price. Now all it takes for a young artist to produce a documentary is an out-of-the-box Mac, a camera, and the will to see an idea through to its resolution. The act of writing has always been a personal pursuit, a concentrated form of thought. And now filmmaking, too, shares that meditative space. The tools are handheld, affordable, no less accessible than a Smith-Corona. You can shoot and edit video, compelling video, on a cell phone.[40]

Remaining aware that many student-authors in US colleges and universities are indeed privileged enough to now carry smartphones makes technical accessibility less of an issue (than it would've been in 2010) toward incorporating video projects into CW curricula. GSIs can consider film and video projects as media in nonfiction's realm while also taking part in shaping cultural thought and artistic consideration.[41]

Another possibility involves showing student-authors how they're what Sara P. Alvarez, Amy J. Wan, and Eunjeong Lee classify as "language architects," having them process ways they already participate in language use, code-switching, and so on. This gets educators thinking about where student-authors might be able to play around with acts of modal "translation," which might mean transforming a flash nonfiction text into a short comic, having student-authors remix alphanumeric text into video, audio, or graphic forms—and which can show them how language use manifests across modes and media and helps them think more about language usage within the dimensions of creativity and production.

I discussed Author's Notes earlier, which I resurface here as also being helpful for student-authors to reflect on the language choices they make in their writing. Especially in literary translation, an Author's Note supplementing a commentary gives me a way to dialogue with student-authors about how and whether their language choices are effectively communicated toward target audiences. This directs the kind of feedback I give them, which serves their revision trajectories toward greater clarity of language use in successive drafts. This isn't confined to acts of literary translation but it also connects to ways student-authors composing projects aside from literary translation can comment on language use through reflection. This leads to deliberately assigning work like Marlina Gonzalez's "Dancing between Bamboos," to inch student-authors toward recognizing how code-switching/meshing can occur in creative writing activity itself. This also opens doors for plurilingual student-authors to learn from (and perhaps imitate) the work of Anzaldúa, Gonzalez, and the like and imagine how their language practices might play out when encouraged to mix and match their language resources—toward considering how such practices don't need to only exist in the confines of an assignment or class project but can affect their overall senses of authorship, creativity, and production.

## Conclusions

Maybe the question of *whether* CW curricula should or shouldn't adopt the previously discussed contexts is less immediate than the question of *how* curricula might become *more* translingual as well as how curricula that remain aware of student-authors' language resources can also help address the issues of language discrimination. For example, questions arising from those like Janelle Adsit in *Toward an Inclusive Creative Writing: Threshold Concepts to Guide the Literary Curriculum* (2017) ask, "How can we expand the possibilities of literary writing as we value multivocality?" and "[h]ow can writers support linguistic diversity?" allowing for greater concentration on CW's translingual potential.[42] Adsit also contextualizes these considerations through Janet Neigh's "Dreams of Uncommon Languages: Transnational Feminist Pedagogy and Multilingual Poetics," noting that Neigh's own (women's studies) pedagogy argues that

> "we must deconstruct the illusion of a monolingual environment" across the disciplines. To do this, we "need to devise strategies to engage different languages in classroom interactions." This might mean assigning bilingual or parallel print textbooks, or asking students to work on translations. It also means putting the relationship between language and power on the syllabus for discussion.[43]

On top of examining ways educators in writing studies and CW have argued for remaining inclusive of translingual audiences and student-authors, I hope the points discussed in this chapter can lead to greater progress in discovering some degree of a creative environment that can pride itself on its awareness of language resources. I do stress that these are "baby steps"—including those steps GSIs can be eager to take with available twenty-first-century means, carrying us into an ability to hold these discussions over multiple channels.

The contexts around how we come to understand language and identity are broad and varied. And I want to reiterate that in continuing to discuss translanguaging in these contexts GSIs must consider more than just those languages that are spoken and heard—ensuring they include language resources like ASL within the context of translanguaging and work toward considering how student-authors are asked to harness composing practices in translingual and anticolonial modes. If GSIs can get a ball rolling toward a look at language practices as communicating beyond just listening, speaking, reading, and writing, this could open doors to conversations about possibilities not just for inclusive communication but for inclusive creative communication—toward which all CW should strive in the twenty-first century.

# Writing Prompts

1. After Marlina Gonzalez's "Dancing between Bamboos or the Rules of Wrong Grammar" draft a translingual (e.g., in "Spanglish," "Franglais,"

Chinglish," and "Taglish") text where another language and English have equal value. Do not italicize non-English words.

2. If translating work from another language into English, compose a commentary essay addressing what makes *you* an effective translator. What is it about your position/identity (e.g., nationality, gender, race, sexual orientation, and religion) that connects you to the source author/material?

3. If your family's language history isn't Anglophone, draft a text imagining what it would be like to reclaim the language(s) of your heritage.

# Notes

1   Using Sara P. Alvarez et al.'s "Translingual Practice, Ethnic Identities, and Voice in Writing," *translingual* here refers to language being "dynamically used and negotiated between language users and the socially reinforced parameters of language discourses" (Alvarez et al., p. 31).

2   Other programs both in and outside the United States might include the following: the American University of Cairo (Cairo, Egypt, Creative Writing in Arabic), the American University of Paris (Paris, France, Creative Writing), Gallaudet University (Washington, DC., English major & writing minor), Hofstra University (Nassau County, NY, MFA in Creative Writing for Writers of Spanish), the Institute of Indian American Arts (Santa Fe, NM, Creative Writing), and more.

3   Haider, Adil. "The Provider Awareness and Cultural Dexterity Toolkit for Surgeons Trial—Full Text View." *U.S. National Library of Medicine*, Brigham and Women's Hospital, July 3, 2018.

4   The poem can be found in Rich, Adrienne. *The Fact of a Doorframe: Selected Poems 1950-2001*. W.W. Norton, 2001.

5   hooks, bell. *Teaching to Transgress: Education as the Practice of Freedom*. Routledge, 1994.

6   I often direct student-authors to the OWL Purdue page "World Englishes: An Introduction," found at https://owl.purdue.edu/owl/english_as_a_second _language/world_englishes/index.html.

7   hooks, p. 172.

8   Ibid., pp. 173–4.

9   I'll use SAE (Standard American English) as a consistent acronym here, perhaps exemplified through white immigrants whose L1 backgrounds don't conform to those English conventions most privileged throughout the United States.

10  Gonzalez, Marlina. "Dancing between Bamboos or The Rules of Wrong Grammar." *How Dare We! Write: A Multicultural Creative Writing Discourse*, 2nd ed., edited by Sherry Quan Lee, Modern History Press, 2022, pp. 63–74. ISBN 978-1-61599-683-4.

11  Ibid., p. 64.

12  The verb *translanguaging* is defined here, according to Christine N. Tardy, as "a common multilingual practice of switching among languages to complete activities that demonstrates languages to operate on a continuum rather than as discrete entities."

13  Gonzalez, p. 68.

14  This is a question left up to not just student-authors but educators/administrators/ program directors who can help oversee the offerings available to those who might wish to complete work in language traditions other than English. I acknowledge the potential administrative headache in the planning that could be involved here, but I still contend this is a direction CW needs to prepare to go in and which can encompass, at the very least, available courses covering multiple and diverse language traditions. (See, for example, Michigan State University's "Second Language: through '202' proficiency requirement in their Creative Writing Concentration:" https://english.msu.edu/ba-in-english-with-cw-concentration.)

15  In "Switching," Benjamin Bailey describes code-switching as "the use of two or more languages in one speech exchange by bi- or multilingual speakers" (Bailey, p. 241). In this chapter I also apply code-switching not just to speech exchanges but also to writing exchanges.

16  Harmon, Kristen. "Writing Deaf: Textualizing Deaf Literature." *Critical Creative Writing: Essential Readings on the Writer's Craft*, edited by Janelle Adsit. Bloomsbury Academic, an Imprint of Bloomsbury Publishing Plc, 2019, pp. 180–6.

17  Ibid., p. 181.

18  See, for instance, Ha Jin's "Deciding to Write in English."

19  Harmon, p. 186.

20  Dai, Fan. "Creative Writing as Education in the Chinese Context." *Creative Writing and Education*, edited by Graeme Harper, Multilingual Matters, 2015, pp. 71–82.

21  Ibid., p. 71.

22  Ibid., p. 72.

23  Ibid., p. 76.

24  Ibid., p. 75.

25  Sánchez-Martín, Cristina. "Beyond Language Difference in Writing: Investigating Complex and Equitable Language Practices." *Writing Spaces:*

*Readings on Writing*, edited by Dana Lynn Driscoll et al., vol. 4, Parlor Press, 2021, pp. 269–80, https://writingspaces.org/?page_id=799.

26  Also see: Horner, Bruce. "Teaching Translingual Agency in Iteration: Rewriting Difference." *Crossing Divides: Exploring Translingual Writing Pedagogies and Programs*, edited by Bruce Horner and Laura Tetreault, University Press of Colorado, 2017, pp. 87–98. JSTOR, www.jstor.org/stable/j.ctt1r6b08q.9.

27  Sánchez-Martín, p. 276.

28  Using Sánchez-Martín's "Beyond Language Difference in Writing" here, we can refer to dialects as "geographical varieties of a language like 'Southern American English' or 'Chicago English'"; sociolects as "all the social traits—often a combination of them, that inform language practices like 'age', profession', 'gender', etc.'" and idiolects as "unique language patterns that are distinctive from everyone else's" (Sánchez-Martín, pp. 272–3).

29  Alvarez, Sara P., et al. "Workin' Languages: Who We Are Matters in Our Writing." *Writing Spaces: Readings on Writing*, edited by Dana Lynn Driscoll et al., vol. 4, Parlor Press, 2021, pp. 1–13, https://writingspaces.org/?page_id =750.

30  Ibid., p. 5.

31  Ibid., p. 11.

32  For more, see: Cunningham, Jennifer M. "African American Language Is Not Good English." *Bad Ideas about Writing*, edited by Cheryl E. Ball and Drewe M. Loewe. West Virginia University Libraries, 2017, pp. 88–92.

33  Brady, Trisha. "Negotiating Linguistic Borderlands, Valuing Linguistic Diversity, and Incorporating Border Pedagogy in a College Composition Classroom." *Assay: A Journal of Nonfiction Studies*, vol. 5, no. 2, 2019, pp. 1–19, https:// www.assayjournal.com/trisha-brady-negotiating-linguistic-borderlands -valuing-linguistic-diversity-and-incorporating-border-pedagogy-in-a-college -composition-classroon-52.html.

34  Ibid., p. 18.

35  In "Postcolonial Translation Theory," Mambrol defines postcolonialism as "generally used to cover studies of the history of the former colonies, studies of powerful European empires, resistance to the colonialist powers and, more broadly, studies of the effect of the imbalance of power relations between colonized and colonizer" (Mambrol n. pag.).

36  Mambrol, Nasrullah. "Postcolonial Translation Theory." *Literary Theory and Criticism*, June 22, 2019, https://literariness.org/2018/01/11/postcolonial -translation-theory.

37  For multimodal options CW educators might also refer to Alexander, Jonathan and Jacqueline Rhodes. *On Multimodality: New Media in Composition Studies.*

Conference on College Composition and Communication/National Council of Teachers of English, 2014; Arola, Kristin L., Jennifer Sheppard, and Cheryl E. Ball, *Writer/Designer: A Guide to Making Multimodal Projects*. Bedford/St. Martin's, 2014; Arola, Kristin L., et al., "Multimodality as a Frame for Individual and Institutional Change." *Hybrid Pedagogy: An Open-Access Journal of Learning, Teaching, and Technology*, 2014, https://hybridpedagogy.org/multimodality -frame-individual-institutional-change/; Brooke, Collin Gifford. *Lingua Fracta: Toward a Rhetoric of New Media*. Hampton, 2009; Eyman, Douglas. *Digital Rhetoric: Theory, Method, Practice*. University of Michigan Press, 2015; Murray, Joddy. *Non-Discursive Rhetoric: Image and Affect in Multimodal Composition*. SUNY, 2009; Palmeri, Jason. *Remixing Composition: A History of Multimodal Writing Pedagogy*. Southern Illinois University Press, 2012; Reiss, Donna and Art Young. "Multimodal Composing, Appropriation, Remediation, and Reflection: Writing, Literature, Media." *Multimodal Literacies and Emerging Genres*, edited by Tracey Brown and Carl Whithaus. University of Pittsburgh, 2013, pp. 164–82; and more.

38   Brenda Miller and Suzanne Paola note, in *Tell It Slant: Creating, Refining, and Publishing Creative Nonfiction* (2012), that "it could be useful to look at this [graphic] form as a model for how we might be able to 'convey an ocean of feeling inside a single image.' You could envision a traditional narrative as a comic strip and allow this visualization to help you hone in on the key details, senses, and gestures that are necessary to bring your story to life. You can try inserting even a single primitive drawing or sketch within a traditional narrative to see how it disrupts and deepens the piece. Or you might collaborate with a talented artist who could envision even a small part of your work within the complexities of visual language" (Miller and Paola, p. 121).

39   Also see Warner, Andy. "On Graphic Narrative." *The Sentences that Create Us: Crafting a Writer's Life in Prison*, edited by Caits Meissner. Haymarket Books, 2022.

40   Bresland, John. "On the Origin of the Video Essay." *Blackbird*, vol. 9, no. 1, 2010, https://blackbird.vcu.edu/v9n1/gallery/ve-bresland_j/ve-origin_page.shtml.

41   As a perhaps useful distinction, Bresland contrasts film as a medium with the essay as a form, discussing not only the functions of each but also the media of film & video and their levels of access being beneficial to producers and audiences. As Bresland notes, "[f]ilm is visual; the essay is not. Film is collaborative; the essay is not. Film requires big money; the essay costs little and makes less. [. . .] Today, to make a small-scale personal film, you can shoot the thing on an inexpensive digital camera and upload it to any number of free

video sharing sites. In '91 you had to hustle for eyeballs. Now, of course, the artist still hustles (post a video in the middle of a digital forest, there's no guarantee it'll make a sound) but those once formidable barriers to entry—obtaining the gear to shoot your film, and getting it in position to be seen—have been leveled by digital technology. As more literary magazines migrate online, editors are discovering that the old genre categories—fiction, nonfiction, poetry—which made perfect sense on the page, no longer do. The Internet is a conveyance of images and sound as well as text, and print media is scrambling to catch up" (Bresland n. pag.).

42  Adsit, Janelle. *Toward an Inclusive Creative Writing: Threshold Concepts to Guide the Literary Curriculum.* Bloomsbury Academic, an Imprint of Bloomsbury Publishing Plc, 2017.

43  Ibid., p. 95.

# Further Reading

Achebe, Chinua. "The African Writer and the English Language." *The Routledge Language and Cultural Theory Reader*, edited by Lucy Burke, Tony Crowley, and Alan Girvin. Routledge, 2000, pp. 427–33.

Alexander, Jonathan and Jacqueline Rhodes. "Direct to Video: Rewriting the Literacy Narrative." *On Multimodality: New Media in Composition Studies*, edited by Jacqueline Rhodes and Jonathan Alexander, National Council of Teachers of English, 2014, pp. 70–104.

Alvarez, Sara P. et al. "Translingual Practice, Ethnic Identities, and Voice in Writing." *Crossing Divides: Exploring Translingual Writing Pedagogies and Programs*, edited by Bruce Horner and Laura Tetreault. Utah State University Press, 2017, pp. 31–47.

Amato, Joe and Kass Fleisher. "Digital Divides? Two Creative Writers Look Askance at Composition Studies." *Creative Writing in the Digital Age*, edited by Michael Dean Clark, Trent Hergenrader, and Joseph Rein, Bloomsbury, 2015, pp. 73–88.

Bassnett, Susan and Harish Trivedi, editors. *Post-Colonial Translation: Theory and Practice.* Routledge, 2005.

Brueggemann, Brenda Jo. "'Writing Insight': Deafness and Autobiography." *American Quarterly*, vol. 52, no. 2, 2000, pp. 316–21. JSTOR, www.jstor.com/stable/30041842.

Canagarajah, A. Suresh. "Negotiating Translingual Literacy: An Enactment." *Research in the Teaching of English*, vol. 48, no. 1, 2013, pp. 40–67. JSTOR, www.jstor.org/stable/24398646.

Clark, Romy and Roz Ivanič. *The Politics of Writing*. Routledge, 2013.

Costanzo, William. "Film as Composition." *College Composition and Communication*, vol. 37, no. 1, 1986, pp. 79–86, https://doi.org/10.2307/357384.

Donahue, Christiane. "Writing, English, and a Translingual Model for Composition." *Composition, Rhetoric, and Disciplinarity*, edited by Rita Malenczyk et al., University Press of Colorado, 2018, pp. 206–24. JSTOR, www.jstor.org/stable/j .ctt2204s1s.13.

Durst, Russel K. "Geneva Smitherman: Translingualist, Code-Mesher, Activist." *Composition Studies*, vol. 42, no. 2, 2014, pp. 55–72. JSTOR, www.jstor.org/stable /43501856.

Giroux, Henry A. *Border Crossings: Cultural Workers and the Politics of Education*. Routledge, 2005.

Hanauer, David Ian. *Poetry as Research: Exploring Second Language Poetry Writing*. John Benjamins, 2010.

Hesse, Douglas. "The Place of Creative Writing in Composition Studies." *College Composition and Communication*, vol. 62, no. 1, 2010, pp. 31–52. JSTOR, www .jstor.org/stable/27917883.

Horner, Bruce. "Teaching Translingual Agency in Iteration: Rewriting Difference." *Crossing Divides: Exploring Translingual Writing Pedagogies and Programs*, edited by Bruce Horner and Laura Tetreault, University Press of Colorado, 2017, pp. 87–98. JSTOR, www.jstor.org/stable/j.ctt1r6b08q.9.

Lamsal, Tika and Hem Paudel. "Beyond the Politics of Despair: Imagining the Possibilities for Change." *JAC*, vol. 32, no. 3/4, 2012, pp. 758–67. JSTOR, www.jstor .org/stable/41709855.

Mambrol, Nasrullah. "Postcolonial Literary Translation Theory." *Literary Theory and Criticism*, June 22, 2019, https://literariness.org/2018/01/11/postcolonial -translation-theory/.

Neigh, Janet. "Dreams of Uncommon Languages: Transnational Feminist Pedagogy and Multilingual Poetics." *Feminist Formations*, vol. 26, no. 1, 2014, pp. 70–92, doi:10.1353/ff.2014.0007.

Niranjana, Tejaswini. *Siting Translation: History, Post-Structuralism, and the Colonial Context*. University of California Press, 1992.

Palmeri, Jason. *Remixing Composition: A History of Multimodal Writing Pedagogy*. Southern Illinois University Press, 2012.

Pattanayak, Anjali. "There Is One Correct Way of Speaking and Writing." *Bad Ideas about Writing*, edited by Cheryl E. Ball and Drew M. Loewe. West Virginia University Libraries, 2017, pp. 82–7.

Reyes, Reynaldo. "In a World of Disposable Students: The Humanizing Elements of Border Pedagogy in Teacher Education." *The High School Journal*, vol. 99, no. 4, 2016, pp. 337–50, www.jstor.org/stable/44075304.

Silko, Leslie Marmon. "Language and Literature from a Pueblo Indian Perspective." *Critical Creative Writing: Essential Readings on the Writer's Craft*, edited by Janelle Adsit. Bloomsbury Academic, an Imprint of Bloomsbury Publishing Plc, 2019, pp. 160–8.

Simon, Sherry. *Gender in Translation: Cultural Identity and the Politics of Transmission*. Routledge, 1996.

Zhao, Yan. *Second Language Creative Writers: Identities and Writing Processes*. Multilingual Matters, 2015.

# 4

# Before and Beyond Genre

## Critically Considering Craft in the Nonfiction Classroom

While a survey of (undergraduate) student-authors might lead to insights about how and why they come to creative writing (CW) when they enter college/university, it may also be safe to assume many of them have already been practicing CW in *some* form before higher education. This has perhaps manifested as a creative outlet during youth or adolescence or maybe as part of their high school curricula. Maybe, they've postured CW as a form of therapeutic expression.

Something student-authors may find as they come to North American higher education is how CW gets structured in courses that give them practice with different genres. Throughout its history in North American higher education (especially in the United States) CW has encouraged student-authors to practice what we call *craft* through developed curricula, which get them working specifically within (a) genre(s). For some student-authors, this becomes a trajectory moving from their undergraduate program/major and then into a graduate program, and many if not most of these programs will focus on student-authors practicing in one genre, especially when asked to compose book-length manuscripts (likely being one fitting neatly within poetry/nonfiction/fiction). As undergraduates, student-authors often complete successive courses in a genre to hone their skills more carefully or gain practice in a selected genre, on top of the potential completion of capstone projects.

The institutional reality of curricular offerings also needs to be considered— those being that some institutions structure/divide CW *by* genre (with student-authors enrolling in courses like "Introduction to Poetry," "Introduction to

Nonfiction," "Introduction to Fiction," for instance, before moving into more intermediate and advanced forms of the genres' specific courses). Another consideration is of the kind of institution that, at the beginning level, combines genres into a course that might instead be called "Introduction to Creative Writing."

Since this chapter confronts student-authors' expectations in CW programs, it also builds on previous cultural dexterity discussions to examine genre and craft in CW education more broadly, as well as the parameters around nonfiction student-authors' education. It focuses on CW's expectation(s) in the "ivory tower" to get graduate student instructors (GSIs) and student-authors together to better reflect on and critique the reasons behind learning to practice CW in the ways they have (i.e., via higher education). As a result, it aims toward a culturally dexterous course outcome like the following: *In this course, student-authors will interrogate the culturally mediated conventions of genre and craft.* This can remain helpful for GSIs bridging gaps between undergraduates in their courses and themselves, who in this reflection study/ practice nonfiction in a North American higher education context.

## Our People, Ourselves

I care about imagining this outcome because my own CW practices have remained connected to US higher education contexts. I have undergraduate and graduate CW degrees and many of the ways I've learned to write in the genres I've practiced (fiction as an undergraduate and nonfiction as a graduate student) were often tied to classroom instruction, especially around assigned readings, course projects, and writing prompts given by instructors over the years. As I've moved into an instructional role myself, I've become allowed to have conversations with student-authors about how they'd like to approach the genre(s) they want to practice—especially when those student-authors come from backgrounds relating to their own understandings of craft, genre, and "good writing."

My own CW education started when I was nineteen during my time as a two-year college student, then continued throughout college and then into my eventual MFA and PhD. I started out practicing in fiction, then worked a bit as a journalist, and then stuck with nonfiction throughout my graduate degrees.

I came to nonfiction through others' stories. Working for an alternative newsweekly, I hopped around my city of residence, learning about the events and interventions people wanted to be highlighted—whether these involved starting literacy programs through bookstores or practicing visual art through ice sculpture. Helping others bring attention to what mattered to them took me away from my own fictions and into others' realities.

This is meant to highlight how student-authors understand CW (here, nonfiction) and the kinds of work they try practicing based on what they've experienced and read. And in terms of reading, when I open a semester, I tend to ask student-authors about any texts they culturally relate to and see how this has influenced their own craft values. How much does it matter that they practice *dialogue*, for instance, or *scene*, or *introspection*, and so on based on the texts they're familiar with? And where do these practices come from regarding student-authors seeing craft choices as integral parts of their own writing?

To keep my nonfiction curricula culturally dexterous, it has remained important to understand notions of both craft and genre as being culturally mediated, on top of attaching these ideas to the craft practices perpetuated by CW's academic environments. Especially because student-authors in my courses, like myself, choose to practice and study CW in higher education, it's important to bridge any gaps between how they're taught to write in higher education contexts with what they've culturally internalized about craft choices.

\*    \*    \*

I've enjoyed discussions about craft and genre with student-authors through Jenny Boully's "On the EEO Genre Sheet." In this essay, Boully intricately parallels (1) how we understand and talk about genre with (2) her own identification, which she ties just as much to genre as to race and ethnicity. Boully begins by stating that "[o]ne of my goals as a teacher of nonfiction is to totally destroy every held belief a student has about essays and nonfiction." She also notes that

> [i]n terms of what I write, it seems that my writing is also mixed. I am sometimes called a poet, sometimes an essayist, sometimes a lyric essayist, sometimes a prose poet. My second book was published under the guise of fiction/poetry/essay.

I find these categorizations odd: I have never felt anything other than whole.

It seems to me that the ability to accept a mixed piece of writing is akin to literary discrimination. I think of the Equal Employment Opportunity (EEO) data sheets: choose the genre that you feel most accurately describes you.[1]

Boully reminds me that maybe part of why I gravitate so strongly toward a text like hers is that she and I have both arrived at different ways of calling our writing and ourselves "mixed." As a student-author I had conversations in workshops about my writing being "too academic" even when the writing also strived to be "literary." My first book is described as a "memoir-in-essays," but I sometimes joke that it's a "memoir with a Works Cited" since I attempted to engage as much with my own perspectives as with others' vantage points as articulated through their texts. So much of this is influenced by my literary heroes like bell hooks and James Baldwin who are, in ways I similarly attempt to be, as often in dialogue as in reflection.

I also aim for "wholeness" in my writing. I can't say I've *always* felt whole around how I describe my writing—I do now, and I like to think this helps me direct student-authors toward feeling whole with their own writing, however they decide to label the writing as we talk about it in our class communities.

Through Boully's work student-authors and I can stay fascinated by how presentations/performances of genre, craft, and self become shuffled—not just around how student-authors are asked to perform in class communities but also in their writing performances through assignments. This can get CW educators to ask student-authors to try defining where they "fit" and to interrogate where they align with how others (e.g., editors and publishers) insist they fit then attempt to proceed toward student-authors trying to produce the best writing they can in class, in accordance with their senses of authorship.

Another helpful entryway into these discussions involves Chris Stark's essay "Crazy." On top of covering issues of US English standardization/grammar, Stark recounts experiences of workshopping part of her first novel *Nickels: A Tale of Dissociation* as a Native author surrounded by many white (particularly cis male) workshop peers. For one, Stark notes how

[i]t seems that for those of us considered "outsiders," we cannot own or define our own writing. Implicit in that is that we are not to tell our own

stories, fictionalized or not. Implicit in that is that we do not get to have stories. We are to listen, be silent, and be awed by the "right way" to tell a story, as defined by those in the ruling class going back to Aristotle. Native writers, specifically, are criticized for not having a climax, for telling stories in a cyclical fashion, for not following that checkmark structure we were taught since elementary school. As a writer, I have experienced this many times, and as a teacher, I have watched my Native students struggle with these issues as well, but without an understanding that it is a cultural difference being expressed through the very structure of their stories. In the classroom, I always bring up the culture of "how to tell a story" or "good writing."[2]

It's crucial that this points to aspects of cultural mediation—the idea that Stark highlights how "good writing" isn't culturally objective and that "good writing" is mediated by the lenses positioned by our own cultural upbringings. It's important to note even figures as "big" as Aristotle here in that, at least in Western societies, his is a name many of us are familiar with, and there are "rules" of written and rhetorical communication that have been passed down through Western/Aristotelean trajectories that can be unfamiliar (even "weird") to student-authors from non-Western traditions.

It's important to remain open to discussing the relationship between genre conventions, cultural difference, and how nonfiction (though not *only* nonfiction) can perform differently through diverse cultural standpoints.[3] Stark's mention of Native stories being "criticized for not having a climax," for example, could resonate with student-authors who feel similarly about the criticism their creative work receives when the work isn't perfectly aligned with the Western conventions we were "taught since elementary school."

It's also helpful that Stark recalls an experience about how

[o]ne day on my way to teach at North Dakota State University I heard an Asian writer discussing the cultural differences between what she called "Asian writing" versus "Western argumentative writing." She said that the linear style taught in Western cultures would be thought of as stupid in Asian cultures. She said an argument paper is written in a cyclical style until the writer arrives at an answer. Even the literary concept of "conflict" is culturally based. Man versus nature. Man versus man. Man versus Self. Man versus Society. This is not "truth." It is not the only way to write, to view the self and the world. It's a viewpoint. An aspect of an individualistic culture in love with the idea of a white, straight, male hero who exerts great strength

and willpower despite all the odds, i.e. despite nature, despite other men, despite his own demons, despite society. It is, in a nutshell, the ideology of manifest destiny, of white male Amerikkka—the outcast hero conquering all. So if you don't belong to a culture that idolizes those traits, or you want to tell a different kind of story, and you want to write, what do you do? Your writing won't be considered by many to be any good. You might even get slammed in some dank classroom somewhere by an overzealous teaching assistant.[4]

I can't emphasize enough here that GSIs should be prepared for conversations with student-authors around the question, "if you don't belong to a culture that idolizes those traits, or you want to tell a different kind of story, and you want to write, what do you do?" I imagine if I'd begun asking questions like this at a younger age, I would've ended up a different kind of author, a different kind of person. I imagine this the way I imagine that if I'd been born closer to my older siblings, I perhaps could've gotten to know any of our three Native great-grandparents. If I'd been older before my Haitian great-grandfather died (I think I was nine?) I could've pushed more questions onto him about Haitian/Caribbean storytelling. I could say the same for asking my paternal great-grandmother about any German or Jewish stories she might've been given while growing up.

As an adult I can now make decisions about the traditions I reach into as I read and hone my writing practices, but I still think it would've been helpful to be able to note all the possibilities around genre and craft and their cultural contexts while my own authorial senses were developing. So, I hope I can in some way now give student-authors opportunities I never received—maybe not in terms of the questions we ask our elders, but certainly regarding how we talk about how craft choices are valued (or are not valued) in class communities, ultimately creating space for craft choices to coalesce with the cultural positions from which student-authors arrive.

## GSI Resources

Student-authors' relationships to their class communities offer opportunity for GSIs to consider a relationship between the genres student-authors are writing in and their target audience(s). This can involve both peer and GSI feedback toward thinking about how audiences may receive the draft in-process, on top of considering practices of rhetorical listening around cultural lack of awareness toward student-authored writing.

It can help GSIs to consider "'Do I Bend Genre? Or Does Genre Bend Me?': Toward an Ageneric Pedagogy," a virtual presentation by Wes Jamison (a doctoral student at the University of Louisiana—Lafayette at the time of the presentation) wherein Jamison discusses links between "genius" and figures like Pablo Picasso, Gertrude Stein, and others—along with their refusal at categorization and how this plays into audiences' perceptions of genius. What's most usable is how Jamison expresses that "any kind of adherence to genre marginalizes voices, authors, and identities" and the ways this echoes what we observe from those like Jenny Boully and Chris Stark.[5]

It may serve GSIs well to notice how adherence and marginalization go hand-in-hand—that is, how adherence to Western traditions can marginalize those from outside these traditions. In the process, CW educators lose opportunities to see work truly flourish from student-authors who'd perform their best by capitalizing on traditions they're most familiar with and that are most native to them—whether the traditions exist outside, for example, the parameters of Standard American English, linear narrative, narrative with climaxes/dramatic arcs, and more.

It's helpful how Jamison reminds us that "genre is not fixed: when we teach what a genre is, it is only a matter of time before we are wrong, without ever having informed our students that genres *do* change and are *not* static."[6] The ways memoir's written has changed, for example: as have the ways journalism has been written, the ways essay forms have adapted and twisted and turned since Michel de Montaigne's naming the *essay* in the sixteenth century. Reminding student-authors of these historical changes can be reassuring for them to know there's as much to learn from John D'Agata's anthology *Lost Origins of the Essay* (2009) as from his *The Next American Essay* (2003). (I mention both here as examples of the transcultural observation of the essay as a form and the conversations around the genre's "changing conventions.")

The thinking around this issue offers GSIs an opportunity to consider "genre normativity" and how this normativity is "monolithic" and "hegemonic" (Jamison) on top of how it can marginalize student-authors arriving from traditions and backgrounds that don't fit "culturally based" (Stark) assumptions. This applies especially to student-authors who strive to innovate based on not only what they've seen but what they've imagined—embracing a creativity that can serve student-authors by steering them toward the kinds of texts they can value within multiple traditions.

Educators can further emphasize that it's OK for student-authors not to be strict with genre, illustrated through Jamison's insistence that

> [i]f we continue to pigeonhole learners (and writers, generally) into strict genre categories, if we limit their writing to these genres, if we continue to treat intergenre and hybrid work as product or descendent of our current genre system, and if we continue to fail to teach that genre is not a category of products but only an ideology, we remain complicit in those hegemonic values.[7]

This gets us back to a focus on creative texts' usability in class communities. Educators need to recognize that what we perceive as "intergenre and hybrid work" isn't new, doesn't necessarily even present ways of composing that we've never seen before but, rather, offers a diversity of options student-authors can learn from—whether in studying Sei Shōnagon or Virginia Woolf.

*   *   *

This connects GSIs to another avenue for encouraging student-authors to practice what's called "critical genre awareness" by way of Amy Devitt's essay "Teaching Critical Genre Awareness." Devitt discusses how, because of educators' obligation to teach genres in their classrooms, they should do so deliberately *with* genre awareness, noting that, at least institutionally, "we must all teach using genres, in the texts we have students read and in the assignments we have students write. Whether we use genres consciously in the classroom or not, the genres we assign promote particular worldviews just as the topics we have them read about do."[8] It's important that as student-authors become entrenched in institutional conceptions of genre, they're also able to note what such an entrenchment means not just around the genre's history or readers' shared knowledge, but also how genres are and have remained tied to the ideologies of those continuing to teach (and write about) genre. Devitt argues that "[a]rmed with genre awareness [. . .] students can distance themselves from the everyday practices of the genres that surround them but also can act, can participate in those genres."[9] This can apply to many CW scenarios—or even simply to the act of reading. Student-authors' being exposed to texts in genre(s) ideally prepares them to better create texts/media like those they envision based on previous exposure—reading screenplays gives future screenwriters ideas about how to write a screenplay, for instance. The same might apply to the short story, the ghazal, the personal essay, the literacy narrative, and so on.

What may be most important is how Devitt notes that as student-authors "take up a genre, they take up that genre's ideology. If they do it *unawares*, then the genre reinforces that ideology. When teachers select genres to use in the classroom, then, they are selecting ideologies that those genres will instill in students, for good and bad."[10] This gets reinforced by use in classrooms of CW "field guides" and "how-to" books, with student-authors potentially being influenced to think from such guides, *This is* always *how [genre X] is done*, rather than examine the context of a genre's history/ies and potential future(s).

Being able to ask student-authors, *What do we do with [genre X] once it has been contrasted within a geographical and historical context,* and *what kind of understanding of [genre x] can we reach through interrogation?* offers thinking that can be repeated for their future courses. This questioning also adopts a contrastive approach, encouraging student-authors to think not "this is how [the] genre *is* done," but rather, "this is how [the] genre *can be* done" through examples gleaned from multiple historicized vantage points.

*    *    *

A final resource for GSIs might come from Wendy Ryden and Danielle Sposato, who argue in "Cultivating Convergence through Creative Nonfiction: Identity, Development, and the Metaphor of Transfer" for using nonfiction to view pedagogy through a kind of gestalt, evaluating student-authors' work alongside their creative exigencies. For instance, the authors write that beyond "outcomes-based assessment" they instead suggest a convergence model as

> a coming together of knowledges with "a polyphony of experiences, inside and outside the classroom" (Nowacek 11) in certain ways within an agent, combining and exceeding the individual contributing factors, to produce plenitude and a sustaining identity. Under this paradigm, development occurs through the affordance of opportunities that exceed any one domain and encompass both classroom and extracurricular experiences; the personal and the social cognition and emotion to effect transformation

through and within "the whole student" (Schoem, Intro 2) in relation with emerging ecological contexts.[11]

GSIs can use a convergence model to view not just how student-authors are asked to compose texts in CW that can lead them toward a career, for example, but at the same time can examine how student-authors learn to write creatively by looking both "forward" and "backward." If one direction views the student-author's future endeavors, then another direction points toward their motivations, knowledges, traditions, and so on, more fully considering what they bring into the class as individuals creating work that often deals with both subjectivity and experience.

In aiming for this, Ryden and Sposato argue for

> an inquiry into development rather than transfer that is less about *tracing* and more about *creating* hospitable conditions conducive to growth and tacit learning. Courses in creative nonfiction, especially as a *method* or *mode* rather than merely genre or craft, may have much to offer in this regard, with an emphasis on the writer's exploration, presentation of self, and relationship to a community engaged in ethical listening.[12]

I appreciate pushing nonfiction toward *method* and/or *mode*, focusing on (1) "the writer's exploration," (2) "presentation of self," and (3) a "relationship to a community engaged in ethical listening" (à la Krista Ratcliffe) all together. Maybe the "writer's exploration" provides ways to foster inquiry alongside expression, just as much as a focus on the "presentation of self" could help them develop the authorial identities they want to present to both target and public audiences.

This can let student-authors more firmly find their footing around genre. Through questioning their "fit" not just by way of exploring their tastes but also by exploring genres' own cultural alignments (think, for example, of all the internet trolls upset about the diverse casting in *Lord of the Rings: The Rings of Power*), student-authors might find their place not just through experimentation but through a kind of reflection.

## Praxis

Toward fostering deeper discussions around nonfiction not just as a genre but as a tool for cultural discussion, I've given student-authors Andrew Bourelle's

"Creative Nonfiction in the Composition Classroom: Rethinking Antithetical Pedagogies," wherein Bourelle distinguishes between "expressivist" and "social-epistemic" pedagogies all while trying to locate a middle ground where nonfiction bridges the two, rather than making them (as Bourelle's title suggests) antithetical. Bourelle moves through different nonfiction examples straddling a line between nonfiction in both "camps," ranging from Joan Didion's work, to Scott Russell Sanders's, to Susan Sontag's, to Sarah Vowell's, to Edward O. Wilson's, and others, displaying how nonfiction reaches beyond expression and toward more socially connected discourses. As Bourelle notes:

> creative nonfiction, such as Sarah Vowell's "Shooting Dad," can be used to satisfy the goals of seemingly antithetical pedagogies. Expressivist and social-epistemic pedagogies are two of the leading composition pedagogies of the past several decades and have often been cast in opposition to one another. Both pedagogies sometimes go by other names, such as experiential or expressionistic (for expressivism) or cultural studies (for social). Expressivism focuses on writing for the self, the voice of the author, and writing as a means of self-discovery; on the other hand, the social-epistemic perspective focuses on public writing, writing to communicate, and writing as a means of social critique.[13]

The way Bourelle lays this out seems at first glance like it might, if just because of the terminology involved, be heavy-handed for undergraduate student-authors. This could be offset through more involved discussion of what the terms mean, however—perhaps involving an educator's presentation clarifying for student-authors what terms like *experiential, expressionistic,* and so on can mean for their writing. When I gave student-authors Bourelle's work and we discussed this "spectrum" in class, I created a Venn diagram for them on the classroom chalkboard. One circle was labeled "Expressivism," while the other was labeled "Social Epistemology." I asked the class to tell me about their own reading experiences not just with Bourelle but of nonfiction texts they were already familiar with.

When filling in the spaces with writing "qualities," in Expressivism's circle student-authors voiced to me to write down "personal experience," "emphasizes 'voice,'" and "writing as a means of discovery." In "Social Epistemology" I then wrote "writing as a means to communicate," "writing for (a) community," and writing as "shared experience." Student-authors communicated how they see nonfiction existing in the overlap of the Venn diagram, which placed (at least on the board) clearer possibilities for writing their own nonfiction.

Student-authors got to consider when one approach or/over another might be helpful for their writing depending on content, form, and target audience(s). Whether this involved writing about the loss of a loved one, an instance of racialized or gendered discrimination, or even a coming-out story, this convergence became tied to student-authors understanding that the nonfiction they compose doesn't need to neatly fit one mode or serve one sole purpose.

It's also helpful for students how Bourelle notes that "despite its personal nature, creative nonfiction writing is meant to communicate, meant to be a window for others to view into the world of the writer. The texts can be written for self-discovery and with a distinct voice, but the writing is also meant to be shared, meant to be part of a public discourse."[14] This seems to imply that, at least beyond writing in forms like the diary or the journal, the nonfiction author does want their work to be seen. To think about this desire for visibility, it can be helpful to get student-authors to consider what it'll mean to share their work, what kind of conversation is created *through* sharing the work, and the kind of dialogue the student-author might envision about their work taking place once they send it out into the world.

This isn't to say all student-authors must have publishing expectations placed on them; in thinking about their work being *potentially* public/published, though, it can help to engage them in considering which conversations their work will start, and among whom. This gets tied to Bourelle concluding that

> we can use creative nonfiction reading and writing assignments to engage our students and help them develop in ways that satisfy both pedagogies. We can erase the myth of antithesis between these pedagogies. Instead of writing for the self *versus* writing for others, think of writing for the self *and* writing for others. Instead of writing as a means of self-discovery *versus* writing to critique society and the language of others, think of writing as a means of self-discovery *and* writing to critique society and the language of others. Instead of personal *versus* public writing, we can think of composition as personal *and* public.[15]

I appreciate the joints (as opposed to a binary) Bourelle sets up between social epistemology and expressivism because Bourelle has repeated the article *and* as opposed to *or*. What I want to carry further with student-authors is the idea that not only can we "think of composition as personal *and* public" but understand that nonfiction (rather than just composition) can do the same. Articulating this position for the class community can get educators to interrogate and reposition how we teach nonfiction as a genre, on top of the expectations student-authors might bring to the genre as they come to learn it—rather than merely needing to parse nonfiction into its different subgenres, such as the essay, memoir, literary journalism, lyric, and so on.

Regardless of subgenre, CW educators can ask questions about how the work we encourage student-authors to do can capitalize on the *and*—how it can benefit themselves as well as (a) target audience(s) and how it can nudge them toward conversations with themselves and with their audiences. CW educators can finally ask how placing considerations of the personal and the public near the foundation of a nonfiction course might work to help student-authors interrogate factors beyond genres/subgenres' "traditional parameters."

## Conclusions

When I began writing this, I thought it would result in an argument for achieving what's outlined in this chapter by effacing issues of craft or genre altogether. What I now imagine as necessary for considering issues of "convergence" in nonfiction pedagogies and class communities might instead involve addressing craft and genre head-on, in a way that acts not just as critical but also as considerate of genres' cultural dimensions.

It's also important to note that CW's (often) genre-centered curricula can involve discussing more than just the development of craft. In *Toward an Inclusive Creative Writing: Threshold Concepts to Guide the Literary Curriculum* (2017) Janelle Adsit points out that *genre* as a CW threshold concept "rejects the notion that good writing requires 'formulaic obedience to rules.' Rather, it introduces the idea of convention—and the purposes that conventions serve in particular genres and writing situations."[16] This isn't to say GSIs typically need to think about "obeying the rules" of a genre but, rather, that maybe they're accustomed to genre conventions *as* literary traditions—a way of insisting that their student-authors must "know the rules before breaking them."

CW curricula hold the potential, according to Adsit, to teach student-authors "genre traditions and the histories that give rise to the genres we write within."[17] (It's easy to align myself with this knowing my own MFA program required a History of the Essay course at its beginning.) But aside from curricula, it might help to just consider how often CW intersects with giving student-authors background knowledge in the literary histories of the genres they study.

There's a whole conversation to be had about how these histories have been canonized and even radicalized. And toward curricular potential, educators can witness student-authors begin to perform inquiries into genre not just by questioning the "rules" of the genre, but how student-authors "fit" within them as they search for the places in CW they learn to call home.

# Writing Prompts

1. Keeping in mind that genres are inseparable from the communities who value them, draft an essay *about* genre itself.
2. In the vein of Jenny Boully's "On the EEO Genre Sheet," draft an essay describing yourself as a genre.

# Notes

1   Boully, Jenny. *Betwixt-and-Between: Essays on the Writing Life.* Coffee House Press, 2018.
2   Stark, Chris. "Crazy." *How Dare We! Write: A Multicultural Creative Writing Discourse*, 2nd ed. Modern History Press, 2022, pp. 50–8. ISBN 978-1-61599-683-4.
3   See, for example: D'Agata, John (ed.). *Lost Origins of the Essay.* Graywolf Press, 2009.
4   Stark, p. 53.
5   Jamison, Wes. "'Do I Bend Genre? Or Does Genre Bend Me?': Toward an Ageneric Pedagogy." *Journal of Creative Writing Studies*, vol. 6, no. 1, article 22, 2021, https://scholarworks.rit.edu/jcws/vol6/iss1/22.
6   Ibid., 3:29.
7   Ibid., 14:25.
8   Devitt, Amy. "Teaching Critical Genre Awareness." *Genre in a Changing World*, edited by Charles Bazerman. Parlor Press, 2009, pp. 337–51.

9  Ibid., p. 338.

10  Ibid., emphasis mine.

11  Ryden, Wendy and Danielle Sposato. "Cultivating Convergence through Creative Nonfiction: Identity, Development, and the Metaphor of Transfer." *Journal of Creative Writing Studies*, vol. 5, no. 1, article 2, 2020, https://scholarworks.rit.edu/jcws/vol5/iss1/2.

12  Ibid., p. 4.

13  Bourelle, Andrew. "Creative Nonfiction in the Composition Classroom: Rethinking Antithetical Pedagogies." *Journal of Teaching Writing*, vol. 27, no. 1, 2012, pp. 37–65.

14  Ibid., p. 53.

15  Ibid., p. 63.

16  Adsit, Janelle. *Toward an Inclusive Creative Writing: Threshold Concepts to Guide the Literary Curriculum.* Bloomsbury Academic, an Imprint of Bloomsbury Publishing Plc., 2017.

17  Ibid., p. 96.

# Further Reading

Fodrey, Crystal N. "Teaching CNF Writing to College Students: A Snapshot of CNF Pedagogical Scholarship." *Assay: A Journal of Nonfiction Studies*, vol. 2, no. 1, 2015, pp. 1–26, https://www.assayjournal.com/crystal-n-fodrey-teaching-cnf-writing-to-college-students-a-snapshot-of-cnf-pedagogical-scholarship-21.html.

Nowacek, Rebecca S. *Agents of Integration: Understanding Transfer as a Rhetorical Act.* Conference on College Composition and Communication of the National Council of Teachers of English, 2011.

Schoem, David. "Introduction." *Teaching the Whole Student: Engaged Learning with Heart, Mind, and Spirit*, edited by David Schoem, Shristine Modey, and Edward P. St. John. Stylus, 2017, pp. 1–16.

St. Amant, Kirk. "Writing in Global Contexts: Composing Usable Texts for Audiences from Different Cultures." *Writing Spaces: Readings on Writing*, vol. 3, pp. 147–61, 2020. https://writingspaces.org/?page_id=431.

# 5

# Beyond Genesis

## A Transcultural Exigency for Research in Creative Writing

Often straddling a line between Creative Writing Studies (CWS) and its neighbors umbrellaed beneath an English studies parent, CWS scholars often find themselves engaged with what it means to combine writing and research. When discussing creativity in creative writing (CW) class communities, as educators it can feel important to talk about how authors, both (undergraduate) student-authors and professional authors alike, can use writing to learn to pay attention to the world.

There should be an insistence on awareness in CW education, and CW curricula must actively encourage student-authors' attentiveness. This isn't to detract from an "art for art's sake" education or from educators who value classrooms with pure creation as their cornerstone; rather, it seems necessary for twenty-first-century CW class communities to stretch beyond genesis. There are ways to do this that involve dialoguing about the world and about how the professional authors undergraduates read and write about engage with the world—and especially how graduate student instructors (GSIs) might incorporate varied perspectives and interventions into the ways student-authors can craft and compose their creative and critical texts.

The last five years alone have given student-authors much to consider, especially when expressed in terms some have classified as "hashtag activism": #AllBlackLivesMatter, #CripTheVote, #MeToo, #DefundThePolice, #ProtectAsianLives, and more may be culminating in so much unearthed during the Covid-19 pandemic and altogether creating a cocoon in which CW educators have been given a chance to burrow. Those in CW must decide how to emerge from here, especially for the sake of student-authors who come to CW deliberately seeking a sense of safety that neighbors an atmosphere of expression.

This chapter discusses how emphasis on research in CW (particularly nonfiction) can move curricula toward more common instances of "cross-cultural knowledge." It not only covers how CW research is an important practice for nonfiction student-authors in particular but stretches further to explore *how* research through a culturally dexterous framework can help achieve the outcomes established by CW curricula that intend for research to refine student-authors' communicative repertoires—specifically in milieus that value cultural inclusion and diversity. And, though it doesn't connect explicitly to any module in the proposed cultural dexterity framework, the chapter nonetheless explores these considerations through envisioning a course outcome like the following: *In this course, student-authors will foster cross-cultural knowledge through developing a creative writing research practice and ethic.*

## In the Room, On the Scene

I care about imagining this outcome because I think I've cared about the place of research in CW since my time as an undergraduate, having had to learn about cultural and geographic nuance and context when writing about real places as settings/environments. When moving away from fiction and into nonfiction this meant learning about the people in those environments and my needing to be more thoughtful than I'd been before about the possibilities of representation.

I wrote a good chunk of my first book in Prague, Czechia, for example. This writing didn't just mean sightseeing and people-watching but rather taking a notebook and a voice recorder into cafés, offices, and even bars as I interviewed my teachers and friends. My paying attention then meant enacting a kind of ethic of care toward portraying a city and its people, done through a gentle marriage of CW practices and dialoguing-as-research. As author Tinu Abayomi-Paul (@Tinu) put it in a tweet, "[i]f you write about another culture, they have to be in the room. / Because people from that culture can tell if they're not. / And it's always in ways that send the message 'we care so little about you that we didn't care to check." (This might be *the* writing advice I consistently give to student-authors.)

In my class communities, one of the ways I've encouraged student-authors to begin thinking about "being in the room" as an act of CW research is through going over with them "Inappropriate Appropriation," transcribed from a PEN World Voices Festival panel conversation between Rick Moody, Chimamanda Ngozi Adichie, Patrick Roth, Tsitsi Dangarembga, Minae Mizumura, Katja Lange-Müller, and Yoko Tawada. The panel discusses not just notions of cultural appropriation in literary writing and how this appropriation might be done "rightly" or "wrongly" but also the ways we can be encouraged as authors to remain attentive to the world(s) we try to write about. For starters, Adichie notes in the conversation that

> [w]hen I read a book about Africa by a non-African, I'm very careful and oftentimes resentful because I think people go into Africa and bend the reality of Africa to fit their preconceived notions. I think the same could be said for writing about women when you're a man, writing about blackness when you're white, and while I think such writing should be done, it requires sensitivity. It's easy to say that we should do whatever we want because we're writing fiction, but it's also important to remember context and to be circumspect.[1]

Even given Adichie's focus on fiction here, an important part of what she notes is culturally attentive creative writing "requiring sensitivity," which offers an opportunity for CW educators to talk with student-authors about what such "sensitivity" might involve—which also means placing considerations of audience on the table. This can get student-authors to envision what their potential audiences may look for as well as what potential publishers have a track record of publishing and not publishing/how this might affect ways a student-author crafts their work toward publication.

Adichie talks about how she "find[s] it particularly curious that here in the United States, there's such a thing as a black [*sic*] section of the bookstore— that it's really about what you look like. If I wrote a book about Poland, for example, I would still end up in the black [*sic*] section of the bookstores. There are still categories."[2] When discussing "categories" with student-authors, especially when they're nonwhite, queer, disabled, and so on, it's good to get them to begin envisioning how they might be categorized themselves (whether categorization is their intention or not) while bringing conversations about publishing and power to the fore.[3] For my own part, I wrote a bit about this in *Island in the City*, stating that

> [w]riting about race as a subject is difficult not because it's hefty but because I have so many biases toward it. I'd very much like *not* to be lumped in with writers considered to have made notable contributions to black [*sic*] and African American literature because I'm not writing about *a* or *the* black [*sic*] experience—I'm not writing *as a* black [*sic*] man. Please remove me from the discourse, because I don't represent anyone but myself.
>
> However, another hurdle of self-representation *within* marginalia is that some readers, inevitably, will feel I represent them as well. It always seems dangerous to write about *othered* groups without fear of *mis*representation, which makes me want to avoid labels even more. What I really want is just a slight inverse of one of [James] Baldwin's own wishes: I want to be a good man and an honest writer.[4]

To be clear, when I wrote this, I was still finding my place on the "scene" of creative writing and was highly anxious about issues like those of self-representation. But much has happened since then—in the time since that book I've learned so much more about how to understand myself and my identity, how to understand my family history, more about how I imagine my family's future, and more about how I get positioned not just as an author but as a professional scholar, community member, relative, partner, and friend. I'm still trying to be a good man and an honest writer.

This offers opportunity for conversations with student-authors in my class communities to consider how their work exists outside the classroom, which might put more pressure on them to consider composing/revision choices toward how their work may get culturally situated. Ultimately, this can help them depart from notions that their writing (especially in nonfiction) must be purely expressivist and that the work will hold some cultural component connected to audiences' perceptions and expectations.

To play with these expectations, one more resource for my class communities comes from Julie Hakim Azzam's "How to Erase an Arab," a flash nonfiction text published in *Brevity: A Journal of Concise Literary Nonfiction*, in which Hakim Azzam deliberately uses news headlines including "Israeli General Says Mission is to Smash P.L.O. in Beirut"; "District Starving in Beirut Battle Gets Food Aid; Early Effort Thwarted"; "Palestinians Exit Lebanon in Droves"; "Car Bomb on West Beirut Street Leaves 25 Dead and 180 Injured";

and "Wrecked by Years of Civil War, Beirut is Rising from the Ashes." Hakim Azzam manipulates headlines by using them as section headers, which are followed by reflective and/or narrative threading that provides audiences insight into parts of the author's experiences. Especially because they begin so many sections with a particular moment in time (e.g., "Seventh grade, social studies" and "Tenth grade, the foyer"), Hakim Azzam's text works effectively with narrative while at the same time remaining in concert with the religious and geopolitical aspects of experience.

Hakim Azzam writes, for instance, that "Palestine is a place where memories and stories are born. *Do I remember Gaza or my grandmother's stories about Gaza?* Palestine is a phantom limb that continues to send pain signals through the nerves."[5] This follows a part of the text where Hakim Azzam recalls their seventh-grade teacher telling them Palestine is not a country: As soon as this statement emerges in the text there's a socio- and geopolitical context to address around a character in the text-making a claim contrary to the author's own lived experience.

Hakim Azzam eventually ends the text stating that "all headlines are from the *New York Times* between 1982–1995," and finishing with a note like this solidifies a use of found language.[6] Where CW educators can go with student-authors from here might be to examine "found language" as a potential technique for creating nonfiction that remains attentive to the wider world. A text like "How to Erase an Arab" gives student-authors opportunity to consider what could result from composing their work using other text (e.g., headlines) while remaining a fun way to consider how to engage with research toward a subject about which a student-author is curious.

## GSI Resources

Accepting research's role can point not just to how initiatives in North American CW programs might be developed toward implementing diverse curricula and material in class communities but also toward student-authors' understanding of research's role in CW in the context of clearer/more explicit cultural attention. Especially in North American colleges and universities, emphases on research can help establish further distinctions between MA/ MFA programs and their PhD counterparts, for example. And as educators,

GSIs can nurture ideas around culturally directed research much earlier for the student-authors in their class communities. To get things started for undergraduates, GSIs might begin by clarifying "research" for them in CW's contexts.[7] A helpful direction can come from Graeme Harper's "Research in Creative Writing," where Harper not only works to try zeroing in on a definition of "creative writing research" but attempts to discern what constitutes research in CW—whether research is part and parcel with the writing being done regardless of genre (e.g., essay collection, historical novel and screenplay) in a class community. Harper makes a case for CW research by discussing what it can offer student-authors engaged in CW practices.

For one, toward defining CW research, Harper notes that an author in CW "engages in, and constructs alongside their creative practice, an active critical understanding of a specific kind. This critical understanding is in part based on a development of a craft, a set of skills that are practical, applied, pragmatic; the creative writer learns what works, and aims to employ this learning."[8] This seems to be about authors studying their respective genres to hone/refine their skills as they more progressively develop authorial senses/identities (e.g., as a "poet," as a "memoirist," as an "essayist," and as a "novelist"). But this should also occur while carrying in hand the "critical understanding" of the genres and forms in which student-authors want to develop a proficiency.

Toward these ends, Harper notes that

> [t]he creative writer researches their sense of critical understanding, "in process," whether prior, during or after the production of a single work, and most directly in relation to immediate or future work, planned, or as yet unplanned. To put it another way, the creative writer is engaged in critical understanding in the same way as a creature in the animal kingdom is engaged in observing, learning, applying, fundamentally in order to ensure their survival. This can be called *responsive critical understanding*, and it is both the purpose and the product of creative writing research.[9]

This is closer to the definition I'd like to home in on: *responsive critical understanding*. Harper's imagining a nonhuman animal in the wild is helpful, especially toward considering student-authors at whatever their skill level, and how so much becomes absorbed for them prior to being internalized, processed, and reproduced by way of artistic production. Student-authors are "observing, learning, [and] applying" the conventions of their craft, as garnered from their instructors and from the texts they read in class and attempt to imitate especially if they're "beginners" in their genres.

It's important to consider "responsive critical understanding" (hereafter, RCU) to direct student-authors toward their own CW research practices. Getting them to know their work isn't just about conducting writing exercises (e.g., imitation) but it's also for them to do the work of witnessing: the work of turning their observations into a kind of notation, which generates/transforms/ develops itself into their working drafts.

Harper offers a few "research proposals" as kinds of exercises toward discerning research's role in CW. (I find myself gravitating toward his "proposal one" over the others: "Human action is a combination of human nature and individual dispositions, individual or group acts, and the structures, institutions and cycles of cultures and societies. Can a creative writer investigate this? If so, how? How is a final piece of creative writing a combination of these factors— or is it?")[10] Especially in nonfiction's case, I explore the idea that an author not only can but must investigate this often. In their writing, nonfiction authors must work toward processing the qualities of "human nature and individual dispositions" as well as "individual or group acts" to articulate senses connected to RCU. With the exception perhaps of those like Aimee Nezhukumatathil or Amy Leach (who both do a fantastic job focusing on nonhuman subjects), nonfiction authors are often engaged in writing about human activity; in doing so, these authors carry themselves beyond witnessing and toward acting as stakeholders in the environments they attempt to convey in their work.[11]

It's not enough to watch, though. I suppose I argue that it's not enough for nonfiction student-authors to perform in ways that serve as solely voyeuristic, contending that they also need to practice ways to act as reporters (though not necessarily implying journalism) and active bystanders. In other words, they must act in roles that not only allow them to embrace RCU senses but also eventually help their target audiences process interpretations of facts, lived experiences, and/or witnessed events. Especially considering the phenomena the last few years have given us to deal with, not only is nonfiction helpful toward getting student-authors to develop senses of RCU but what they do develop may even thrive in practices that could be refined in the introductory and intermediate courses they take with GSIs.

Likewise, in "Creative Writing Research" Harper also notes that developing RCU in CW implies "exploring the actions, artefacts and contexts of creative writing, though not necessarily always undertaking creative writing itself."[12] This focuses on aspects like "subjects themes, forms or structures employed in creative writing [. . .] across cultural or linguistic boundaries, differences of gender, race, or sexual orientation, among numerous others."[13] This evokes an importance toward how student-authors choosing to engage in CW research (when they practice CW in college/university settings) can create knowledge "across cultural or linguistic boundaries, differences of gender, race, or sexual orientations," that is, with diverse readerships in mind. In other words, the nonfiction class can be a site where GSIs ask student-authors to engage in research toward responding to cultures and identities different from their own.

GSIs can also benefit from a look at Emma Howes's and Christian Smith's work in "'You Have to Listen Very Hard': Contemplative Reading, *Lectio Divina*, and Social Justice in the Classroom," which helps frame conversations with student-authors about what pedagogically occurs—displaying an insistence that educators think in their class communities about how to offer transcultural attention to authors from outside a Western purview/routine reading by way of course design.

Howes and Smith help show how two instructors work through/attempt to enact antiracist pedagogy in their nonfiction courses (particularly through James Baldwin's *The Fire Next Time* and Ta-Nahesi Coates's *Between the World and Me*) and coaching students through techniques like Richard E. Miller's "slow reading" and Krista Ratcliffe's "rhetorical listening."[14] In doing so, student-authors become more able to see how the racially focused texts they engage with shouldn't be so easily dismissed—that is, they don't merely brush off claims authors like Baldwin and Coates make, trying to eliminate student reactions like "that happened 50 years ago, and we've made a lot of progress since then." As the authors note, this isn't just a matter of enacting antiracist curricula but is also a matter of fully retooling their course readings.[15]

For Bernice M. Olivas, meanwhile, bringing a study of identity into the fold in their own class communities reveals possibilities for GSIs to lead student-authors toward what, for some, might be seen as a lofty goal: alleviating fear of the racialized/sexualized/gendered/etc. "other." In the vein of Mary Rose O'Reilley, who in *The Peaceable Classroom* (1993) had asked the question, "Is it possible to teach English so that people stop hating each other?,"[16] Olivas also asks, "Is it possible to teach writing so that people stop fearing each other?"[17]

Olivas focuses on student-authors in their course learning two things: (1) "How to read from a place of believing rather than a place of criticism in order to better empathize with voices that may challenge our worldviews" and (2) a writing process

> that inquires into our relationships with ourselves and with others who are not like us and the power that helps define those roles. We will write about our relationship to our communities, institutions, and governing bodies. We attempt to locate exigency in our own relationships to power, our communities, our institutions, and our governing bodies.[18]

One way Olivas executes these objectives is by shifting authority to student-authors through asking them to lead discussions, which they note "allows for the opportunity to create new knowledge—things come up in discussion that I can't always anticipate or know."[19] Olivas uses inquiry over analysis as a mode of learning throughout the course, noting that since "human identity is so complex and varied, inquiring into contextualized identity offers nearly limitless points of entry into writing practices that encourage writers to think about larger social issues."[20]

Using any of these, research practices in CW might become central to what GSIs often refer to as "reflexive" or "critical" components of the assignments/projects they give their student-authors, executed *as* responsive critical understanding. RCU can encourage student-authors to anticipate the reactions of their target audiences as well as establish links that, as some argue, pertain to how student-authors come to grasp associations between texts and the societies texts inhabit and represent.

## Praxis

In my courses (especially at the introductory level), one way to encourage transcultural attention/RCU senses via student-authors' CW research has been by giving them assignments/projects that ask that they combine experience and response. Once the class community has reached a research unit/portion of the course, I assign them work like what follows:

> [T]his project is designed to allow you to compose *either* a piece of medium-length (1500–2500 words) researched literary nonfiction, based on a writing

prompt (listed below) *or* a literary translation project (three to five poems, accompanied by a 1200–3600-word commentary essay).

*Researched Literary Nonfiction:*

- Prompts:
  - Draft a literary/creative nonfiction text utilizing research on immigration in the United States.
  - Draft a text that is helpful to the #AllBlackLivesMatter movement.
  - Draft a text that is helpful to survivors of sexual violence.
  - Draft a text using research on an environmental or public health crisis within the last five years.
  - Draft a text exploring a dialect or language policy in a particular environment (e.g., in public schools).
  - Draft a text focused on an issue in a specific geography outside the United States.

With these options student-authors have an opportunity to gravitate toward the issues/causes closest to them. Student-authors coming from plurilingual backgrounds might pursue the option on language policy, for instance; likewise, a student-author interested in climate issues might compose a text focused on an aspect of environmental justice. This gives student-authors a chance to fuse genuine interest with ways to learn more about how to engage with the conversations *around* those interests—especially when these interests connect to broader environments, this can encourage nonfiction's social-epistemic potential. It results in a kind of "writing to learn" for nonfiction student-authors, allowing them a chance to engage with ways other authors process issues close to their hearts through public spheres.

Student-authors can also choose to embark on a literary translation project, which I describe for them as follows:

> [I]n this project you must keep in mind the ways content, form, and notions of anticolonial translation come together in your translation. (Use course readings for reference.) Begin by searching for three to five poems you've chosen to translate, then accompany your translations with an articulation of your translation choices in a 1200–3600-word commentary essay.

The student-authors I've seen most eager to undertake the literary translation option are those coming from plurilingual backgrounds who might have a favorite author in their L1 whose work they'd love to translate into English. (I've also seen student-authors with study abroad experience try working with authors they've discovered in the countries they've visited.) The translation option results in capitalizing on a convergence of student-authors' knowledges, which sometimes comes from newly developed thoughts and ideas and other times emerges from the ideas with which they've already been engaging awhile. Especially for the plurilingual student-authors who have favorite authors in their native languages, this offers them opportunity to consider both the challenges and the ethics of bringing the text into English to share a love for an author's work with those who may otherwise never encounter it.

Finally, instructions my student-authors receive for both project options are delivered as follows:

*Instructions for Option #1*: Begin by selecting a news article (don't use a feature story, however) related to your chosen prompt from the previous list. Compose your draft by first summarizing any narrative details in your own words. That is, make your source text more elaborate/vivid through your own rhetorical choices and considerations. Finally, consider: What is it about this event/situation that stands out to you as the researcher? What's your reason for choosing this topic?

*Instructions for Option #2*: Similar to the trot exercise introduced in class, begin by creating your own trot from your selected author's source text. Your first draft should encompass both the trot and your translation together—eventually working toward a fuller collection (of three to five poems) alongside your commentary-essay.[21]

With the instructions given for either option, student-authors become able to think beyond themselves. They begin their CW research endeavors by engaging externally generated issues/texts, then discern how to internalize the process of refining their connections to these issues/texts. This connects them to RCU senses by especially having them consider ways of ensuring their drafts begin opening doors to broader conversation—whether such conversation is around environmental issues or why a certain South African, Brazilian, Japanese (etc.) author should be read more widely in English.

Once student-authors (and student-translators) begin to undertake this connective work, the class community reaches a place where not only does everyone further their own learning, but they also encourage others' learning processes along the way. In the end, this carries class community members to a place where they develop deeper understandings not only around the texts that get shared but in the process; they become better able to "read" one another, as well.

# Conclusions

Understanding CW practices as needing, according to Janelle Adsit in *Toward an Inclusive Creative Writing: Threshold Concepts to Guide the Literary Curriculum* (2017), to involve "specific modes of attention as writers learn to be close and critical observers of the world," authors must also "learn to account for the ethical considerations involved in perceiving and reinventing the world through their research and observation."[22] Student-authors must learn in their nonfiction, fiction, poetry, screenwriting, and so on to converse, rather than to merely express. This can become central to our CW pedagogies, encouraging student-authors toward an awareness of transcultural discourses so much different from their own. As they work toward creating literary work that's informed and not just imagined, they display efforts toward thoughtful representations of the many cultures and identities they access through reading and writing.

I hope student-authors can consider the worlds beyond their front yards and back yards. I know many already do, but if I might push them further, then it may introduce them not only to ways they can widen their own ambitions but also how they can shape the conversations taking place in their class communities, at writing conferences, in journals and anthologies, and so on, which may be open to such cross-talk.

# Writing Prompts

1. Draft a text about a vacation you took. What does it mean for you to be the author representing this locale to your audience? (Who *is* your audience?) Mention two colors.
2. Provide a recipe for a dish/food item from your heritage. As you detail how the dish is prepared, also provide its history, letting the audience know about its cultural and historical significance. Mention the kind of weather the dish would best be consumed in.

3. Draft a letter centering yourself in an historic event you've lived through. Deliberately imagining an audience different from yourself, provide context for the audience to clearly understand the event.
4. Draft a text around a story you heard or read about in the news, but that you can't stop thinking about. (Why can't you stop thinking about it?)

## Notes

1 Moody, Rick et al. "Inappropriate Appropriation." *Critical Creative Writing: Essential Readings on the Writer's Craft*, edited by Janelle Adsit, Bloomsbury Academic, An Imprint of Bloomsbury Publishing Plc, 2019, pp. 200-9.
2 Ibid., p. 207.
3 Also see: Older, Daniel José. "Diversity Is Not Enough: Race, Power, Publishing." *Literary Publishing in the Twenty-First Century*, edited by Travis Kurkowski et al., Milkweed Editions, 2016, pp. 154–63.
4 McCrary, Micah. *Island in the City: A Memoir*. University of Nebraska Press, 2018.
5 Hakim Azzam, Julie. "How to Erase an Arab." *Brevity: A Journal of Concise Literary Nonfiction*, September 12, 2016, https://brevitymag.com/nonfiction/how-to-erase/.
6 Ibid.
7 A focus to borrow from a writing studies angle contrasts *research* with *scholarship*. "In writing studies," as Katrina M. Powell writes in her entry for *Keywords in Writing Studies* (2015), "the terms *research*, *scholarship*, and *inquiry* are often used interchangeably, evoking a sense of informed study around a topic from a particular theoretical stance" (Powell, p. 155). Scholars in writing studies often then imply that *scholarship* is empirical "as opposed to rhetorical research or inquiry," though "many scholars in the field see their research as doing both" (155).
8 Harper, Graeme. "Research in Creative Writing." *Teaching Creative Writing*, edited by Graeme Harper, Continuum, 2006, pp. 158–71.
9 Ibid., p. 162.
10 Ibid., p. 170.
11 See: Amy Leach's *Things That Are: Essays* (2014) and Aimee Nezhukumatathil's *World of Wonders: In Praise of Fireflies, Whale Sharks, and Other Astonishments* (2020).
12 Harper, Graeme. "Creative Writing Research." *Key Issues in Creative Writing (New Writing Viewpoints)*, edited by Dianne Donnelly and Graeme Harper, Multilingual Matters, 2012, pp. 103–15.

13  Ibid., p. 108.

14  Howes and Smith note that Miller's "Reading in Slow Motion" resulted in a curriculum "that allowed for the slow reading of one entire work over the course of the semester and to have students practice reading as an opportunity for reflection and meditation" (Howes and Smith, p. 12). Meanwhile, Ratcliffe's *rhetorical listening* equates to "more than simply listening for our own self-interested intent, which may range from appropriation (employing a text for one's own ends), to Burkean identification (smoothing over differences), to agreement (only affirming one's view of reality). Instead, understanding means listening to discourse not for intent but with intent—with the intent to understand not just the claims, not just the cultural logics within which the claims function, but the rhetorical negotiations of understanding as well" (Ratcliffe, p. 205).

15  They've noted a transparent exigence in the classroom for such readings, noting that "[t]he need to rethink not only our curriculum, but our pedagogical approach to race and social justice more broadly, was incredibly clear. In order to move towards an anti-racist classroom space, we not only had to strive to broaden the voices and perspectives available to our students, but to consider ways to move students through the experiences these voices represented. We remained committed to the use of non-fiction texts as the basis for these goals, but had to more deeply consider the pathways we encouraged our students to explore" (Howes and Smith, p. 3).

16  O'Reilley, Mary Rose. *The Peaceable Classroom*. Boynton/Cook Publishers, 1993.

17  Olivas, Bernice M. "Politics of Identity in the Essay Tradition." *Assay: A Journal of Nonfiction Studies*, vol. 2, no. 1, 2015, pp. 1–29, https://www.assayjournal .com/bernice-m-olivas-politics-of-identity-in-the-essay-tradition65279-21 .html.

18  Ibid., p. 8.

19  Ibid., p. 10.

20  Ibid., p. 12.

21  A *trot* serves as a word-for-word translation of the source text, which then asks student-translators to begin the work of changing these trots into more poetic/ prosaic forms that result in (translated) target texts.

22  Adsit, Janelle. *Toward an Inclusive Creative Writing: Threshold Concepts to Guide the Literary Curriculum*. Bloomsbury Academic, an Imprint of Bloomsbury Publishing Plc., 2017.

# Further Reading

Bailey, Christine and Patrick Bizzaro. "Research in Creative Writing: Theory into Practice." *Research in the Teaching of English*, vol. 52, no. 1, August 2017, pp. 77–97.

DiAngelo, Robin. "White Fragility." *International Journal of Critical Pedagogy*, vol. 3, no. 3, 2011, pp. 54–70.

Elbow, Peter. "The Believing Game—Methodological Believing." *The Journal of the Assembly for Expanded Perspectives on Learning*, vol. 5, 2008, https://scholarworks .umass.edu/eng_faculty_pubs/5.

Giroux, Henry. *Border Crossings: Cultural Workers and the Politics of Education.* Routledge, 1992.

Miller, Richard E., director, *Reading in Slow Motion: The Humanities and the Work of the Moment.* YouTube, July 26, 2017, www.youtube.com/watch?v=gHLSKfQyRyw.

National Council of Teachers of English, director. *"Funk, Flight, and Freedom"—2015 CCCC Chair Adam Banks' Address.* YouTube, March 24, 2015, www.youtube.com/ watch?v=EYt3swrnvwU.

Older, Daniel José. "Diversity Is Not Enough: Race, Power, Publishing." *Literary Publishing in the Twenty-First Century*, edited by Travis Kurkowski et al., Milkweed Editions, 2016, pp. 154–63.

Powell, Katrina. "Research." *Keywords in Writing Studies*, edited by Paul Heilker and Peter Vandenberg, Utah State University Press, 2015, pp. 155–9.

Ratcliffe, Krista. *Rhetorical Listening: Identification, Gender, Whiteness.* Southern Illinois University Press, 2005.

"Research Statement." *Creative Writing Studies Organization*, April 13, 2020, https:// creativewritingstudies.com/creative-writing-studies-research-statement/.

Selasi, Taiye. "Stop Pigeonholing African Writers." *Critical Creative Writing: Essential Readings on the Writer's Craft*, edited by Janelle Adsit, Bloomsbury Academic, An Imprint of Bloomsbury Publishing Plc, 2019, pp. 46–53.

# 6

# Toward Critical Concepts in the Nonfiction Classroom

## Some Reflections on Course Designs

### Course Description: Introduction to Creative Nonfiction

In addition to writing-intensive practice in literary/creative nonfiction, this course also involves an introduction to threshold concepts in creative writing (nonfiction) by examining authors' cultural, professional, institutional (including those in academic environments), and theoretical concerns. This class will help beginning student-authors hone their literary practices through reading and composing creative nonfiction through culturally dexterous lenses, specifically through a survey of global nonfiction and/or literary translation.

Considering the elements of brief creative nonfiction (and considering examples covered as a class) discussed throughout the first unit of the course, the first major project asks student-authors to compose a "flash" (700–750 words) nonfiction text. Using course readings as potential models, the flash nonfiction project will allow student-authors to explore reflection and personal experience within a short form.

The second project/unit is designed to allow student-authors to compose either a medium-length (1,500–2,500 words) researched creative nonfiction text based on a writing prompt (listed on the project assignment sheet) *or* a literary translation project (three to five poems) accompanied by a commentary essay.

A third project in the course asks student-authors to survey the landscape of literary publishing, resulting in a 250–300-word publication "write-up" displaying the student-author's familiarity with a chosen literary journal, magazine, anthology, and so on. The write-up will also note the publication's history, and how such history intersects with acts of inclusion and/or marginalization.

In a final portfolio/project, student-authors will revise any work they choose (from writing prompts/workshopped writing/major projects) from throughout the course, an additional requirement being that they *target a specific publication of their choice* (the class will be provided a list of options). Considering the threshold concepts and readings from throughout the course, the second part of the portfolio then asks student-authors to respond to two (2) exam questions in the form of short (700–750 words) papers using course readings as illustrations/examples.

## Course Description: Studies in Creative Nonfiction

How might we utilize literary/creative nonfiction as a tool to explore our and others' social identities? How can studying and practicing creative nonfiction forms help address the conditions affecting people from minoritized and/ or marginalized identities? To explore these questions and more, this course surveys a selection of texts pointed toward the numerous cultural exigencies surrounding creative nonfiction. The authors surveyed in the class will focus on lived experiences of racism, sexism, ableism, and so on—particularly toward utilizing memoir and the essay to investigate the intersection between identity, power, and social bias(es).

The first unit will result in a "flash" (700–750 words) nonfiction (essay or memoir) text asking student-authors to focus on detailing the first realizations of an aspect of their identity. This could include but not be limited to their racialized identities, gendered identities, disabled/nondisabled identities, sexual orientations, income levels, regional/geographical identities, generational identities, and so on.

The second unit will focus on student-authors composing an "Identity Notebook." In a medium-length (1,500–2,500 words) text, student-authors will address questions from David Mura's *A Stranger's Journey* to explore their identities through history—particularly family history in contrast to their own lived experiences.

In the last unit, student-authors will revise any work they choose (from writing prompts/workshopped writing/major projects) from throughout the course into a final portfolio, along with a reflection detailing how texts produced and/or consumed throughout the course have affected their considerations of the relationship between identity and creative nonfiction.

## Institutional Context

As a four-year private research university located on Haudenosaunee ancestral lands in central New York, Syracuse University (SU) serves 21,772 undergraduate, graduate, and law students at its main campus in what is now Syracuse.[1] As of a fall 2021 census, SU comprises 11,407 white students alongside 6,675 nonwhite students (classified by SU as "American Indian or Alaska Native," "Asian," "Black or African American," "Hispanic or Latino," "Native Hawaiian or Other Pacific Islander," and "Two or more races"), with the major nonwhite populations being "Hispanic or Latino" (2,129), "Black or African American" (1,616), and "Asian" (1,377). Other demographic categories include "Nonresident Alien" (3,690) and "Race/ethnicity unknown" (609).

My first attempts at Introduction to Creative Nonfiction/Studies in Creative Nonfiction courses were taught to SU student-authors throughout 2019–22 and were foundationally adapted from a sample syllabus included in the Appendix of Janelle Adsit's (Humboldt State University) *Toward an Inclusive Creative Writing: Threshold Concepts to Guide the Literary Curriculum* (2017). I note here that while Adsit's syllabus is based on critical and transcultural readings, they also focus heavily on fiction/fiction writing practices. My course designs have instead adapted Adsit's threshold concepts toward course outcomes for literary/creative nonfiction, for example, flash nonfiction, memoir, and the essay, by not just introducing student-authors in the course to transcultural readings in literary nonfiction but also providing them an introduction to creative writing (CW) as a profession in addition to critical thinking around CW as an academic subject.

My course designs hadn't existed yet at SU; and, being foundational to my own pedagogical work, the courses have served as a kind of summit for where my research and scholarship have meant to lead. With this work culminating in sample course designs for nonfiction at different levels, the designs have asked student-authors to develop their practices through the reading/ discussion/imitation of transcultural nonfiction literature and craft-criticism (as a kind of "writing about creative writing"). This has also built on the work of writer-researchers/CW educators covering topics ranging from race and gender in creative writing, to language attitudes in CW, to institutionalized CW practices, and more, expanding student-authors' considerations of how published creative writing intersects with culture and audience—in turn, encouraging them to consider how their own identities, discourses, values, and so on have impacted their CW practices.

Given the makeup of my campus environment and given that no courses with such explicit designs had previously existed within departmental curricula, the designs here have offered student-authors opportunities to bridge their CW interests with culturally critical conversations at different curricular levels. Especially intended to be a kind of makeover for normative workshop courses often found at North American institutions of higher education, courses like these have attempted to set themselves apart by focusing not just on threshold concepts but also on CW scholarship around writing cultures/practices, via the perspectives of a diverse set of nonfiction authors and course readings. Additionally, while these courses have contained workshop components, they have not *centralized* the workshop model—which overall offers student-authors nuanced angles from which to evaluate their CW practices, while also asking them to develop a critical consciousness informed by (and not necessarily isolated from) core texts introduced throughout the courses.

Perhaps most centrally, the university's makeup, coupled with its location, has provided an impetus for discussions around cultural dexterity in CW classrooms. That is, a campus that's approximately 65 percent white (discounting "Nonresident Aliens" and "Race/ethnicity unknown") has especially warranted dialogues that might provide student-authors a departure from typically canonized (i.e., often authored by racially/linguistically privileged persons fitting into dominant discourses) readings, so that curricula can be adapted toward other North American campuses where student-authors taking introductory courses can combine CW study with cultural exchange.[2] I'd also never had so many international student-authors before joining SU, and these circumstances encouraged me to think more deeply about the multitude of traditions being brought into my classroom—preparing me overall to discuss literary values and conventions I may have otherwise been unfamiliar with.

In the following I outline the attempts to refine these course designs specifically in the context of my home institution, ultimately leading toward a template that could be used by graduate student instructors (GSIs) learning to teach their own introductory and intermediate nonfiction courses.

## Scholarly Rationale

The introductory course finds its base in Janelle Adsit's article "The Writer and Meta-Knowledge about Writing: Threshold Concepts in Creative Writing," which "proposes 12 threshold concepts for creative writing that emphasize aesthetic sensitivity, the diversity of the textual landscape, historical knowledge of craft traditions, and the complexities of the writing process."[3] Rather than ask student-authors to focus only on the article, I instead ask that they remain attentive to the CW threshold concepts laid out by Adsit and covered throughout the course. In arranging these concepts, meant to "fundamentally transform a learner's practice, sense of themselves and the world, and/or way of knowing" they're spread throughout our course calendar, covering approximately one concept per week.[4] I've rearranged Adsit's threshold concepts in my own course schedule out of what I've seen to be an urgency for certain concepts being introduced to student-authors in a particular order.

Another rationale for the introductory course emerges from a belief in Adsit's work being significant enough to warrant exploration not just throughout the space of an article or book chapter (though Adsit of course expands the threshold concepts in *Toward an Inclusive Creative Writing: Threshold Concepts to Guide the Literary Curriculum*, 2017) but believing it deserves its place in an entire CW curriculum—both for new student-authors at the undergraduate level learning how to participate in CW's communities of practice and also for graduate student instructors (GSIs) developing their CW teaching philosophies and discerning how to articulate such philosophies through their own developing pedagogies.

What might also be important to note is positioning the course as an introductory survey for non-majors: while Adsit's demographic seems to comprise student-authors already majoring in CW/English and their developing literary practices in fiction, I've hoped for the introductory course to also open a space for discussion that involves student-authors who don't all yet necessarily identify as "creative writers"—also leading to reflection on how they've benefited from the pedagogies/course designs more broadly within their majors.

As I already mentioned, stretching Adsit's threshold concepts out over the course of a semester allows for movement through every concept weekly, by pairing them with texts I believed might best highlight what I've understood to be the concepts' core ideas. Operating on brief descriptions Adsit provides, student-authors and I are then able to examine how the concepts become effectively attached to the readings we discuss together as a class community.

A second foundation for the introductory course then comes from Sherry Quan Lee's *How Dare We! Write: A Multicultural Creative Writing Discourse* (2022) and is pointedly used as a text to give to Intro student-authors, in conjunction with Adsit's article on CW threshold concepts. When used together, both texts allow student-authors to begin their CW educations (at least in nonfiction) by considering nonfiction transculturally—not just in terms of examining aspects of US American nonfiction but noting all the ways authors have come to nonfiction from such varied and different directions.

Part of the support for using Lee's anthology comes from her own exigence for the anthology itself. For one thing, Lee writes that

> [a]s a poet and memoirist and a creative writing teacher in academia and for community organizations, I have asked for years: Where are the textbooks by writers of color about the craft of writing? A text that would address the experiences and needs of writers of color whose work has been/is being silenced, ignored, and recklessly criticized; writers who have been vocally undermined, or on the other hand, patronized.[5]

Intro student-authors might be able to rapidly identify with and connect to this. Especially when some of them come to CW as an area of practice and study as a way not just to fulfill their needs as authors but also to see themselves reflected as readers. Whether for nonwhite student-authors, plurilingual student-authors, queer student-authors, or others, Lee's anthology has been a helpful starting point for those who haven't engaged with nonfiction before. Especially since so many of the essays Lee includes in the anthology serve as kinds of "writing about creative writing," the anthology encourages student-authors to consider "craft" from Day One. And not just *craft* but also the ways craft is mediated by our identities and by our personalized (rather than only creative) exigencies.

Lee also writes about how "[w]hen I began my journey as a creative writer, I noticed there were no books about me—a Chinese Black female who grew up passing for white in Minnesota. So, I began to write myself into existence."[6] This returns to the notion of seeing oneself reflected. The ways Lee had needed to "write [herself] into existence" is something I've witnessed in so many student-authors—student-authors who unfortunately feel as though they're the only ones who *can* represent themselves, those who don't see themselves reflected enough in the literature they've been given by their teachers to read, all trying to locate spaces for the discourses around their identities by writing themselves *into* such discourses. If I were to have a student-author of my own who was, like Lee, a "Chinese Black female who grew up passing for white in Minnesota," I imagine that the CW space would feel somewhat infiltrated on their part—especially in that they'd probably not enroll in the course expecting to engage with work by someone from their own specific identity. An anthology like Lee's can then get student-authors excited to begin their study of nonfiction by not only engaging with so many of nonfiction's culturally situated vantage points but also, potentially, locating motivations toward writing their own selves into existence.

Lee finally notes:

> I believe who we are influences our writing; just as who we are may defy those who think they have power over our writing. I knew in my heart that for writers of color, writing isn't just about process and craft, but also the challenges we face as writers, and how we overcome those challenges. I imagined a textbook that gives support and encouragement to those of us who understand that one size doesn't fit all, that MFA programs don't necessarily address our needs, nor do publishers necessarily accept stories that don't fit their agendas or economic needs. I wanted a textbook that considers the relevance of race, class, gender, age, and sexual identity; culture and language; and that by so doing, on some level, facilitates healing.[7]

Though student-authors at the introductory level aren't necessarily already thinking about graduate programs, they are already thinking about "the relevance of race, class, gender, age, and sexual identity; culture and language," and more. So, the texts Lee has included in the anthology help point to different ways these identities become addressed by way of nonfiction. The diversity of the authors Lee has published are conversation-starters that also serve as invitations—invitations for student-authors to engage in discussions about the subjects that may already be on their minds, but which they haven't yet figured out how to discuss.

A last thing to note about Lee's anthology is how foundational it truly has been in its use at the introductory level—encouraging student-authors to recognize that, as Lee writes, "for writers of color, writing isn't just about process and craft, but also the challenges we face as writers, and how we overcome those challenges."[8] This isn't to say I hope student-authors *only* think about their challenges/difficulties and having to overcome obstacles and barriers; what I hope they come to know is that, if they do wish to have these conversations, then they aren't alone. Many other authors in nonfiction are trying to have the same conversations. And so, Lee's book has overall been amazing to use at the introductory level—I hope it's just the beginning of what Lee's very subtitle notes as being a "multicultural creative writing discourse."

I've utilized the resources already mentioned toward the introductory syllabus not just in an attempt to tailor them to nonfiction but also to highlight how both Adsit's threshold concepts and Lee's selections might help to position student-authors' perspectives toward nonfiction's cultural potential. In the end, I hope both resources have prepared introductory student-authors to recognize nonfiction not just as a potentially creative endeavor but as a vehicle toward greater understanding of themselves and others.

✳    ✳    ✳

I've meanwhile designed "Studies in Creative Nonfiction" around David Mura's book *A Stranger's Journey: Race, Identity, and Narrative Craft in Writing* (2017) to prepare student-authors for conversations stretching beyond just an "introduction to the field" (à la "Introduction to Creative Nonfiction"). The Studies course exists at the 400-level at my home institution, so it often consists of student-authors already coming into the course with previous CW experience. Perhaps some student-authors are fulfilling curricular requirements across genres, while perhaps others are at a stage of their undergraduate careers where they've begun thinking about graduate CW study.

A book like Mura's doesn't just helpfully theme the course but it also gets student-authors to evaluate (and reevaluate) their own approaches to CW practices as intersected with their identities. As Mura states in his Introduction,

[t]he purpose of this book is to instruct writers about their craft, particularly fiction writers and writers of memoir as well as creative writing teachers. In composing the book, I've considered how writers of color have altered our literary tradition and the ways writers practice their craft. One key shift has involved an increased focus on the issues of identity.[9]

These "issues of identity" are broader than merely those issues of racialized identity. Of course, I talk with my student-authors constantly about racialized and ethnic identity, as I get them to consider what it may mean for them to be a "Jewish writer," an "Italian writer," a "South African writer," and so forth on their own terms. This helps us not only prepare for class community discussions around those identities that have been racialized but also consider those existing outside of race and racialization. This allows for conversation around chronic illness, disability, gender identity, and so on and encourages student-authors to engage in perhaps their first thinking around how to put these subjects into writing (by way of class assignments).

Another reason I've chosen to structure the Studies course around Mura's book is the way he states that

[o]verall, this book departs from creative writing books that leave the issues of race and ethnicity beyond the boundaries of how creative writing is taught. My aim here is to broaden the essential elements of the writer's craft. This book is for both writers of color and white writers, for it addresses issues of identity that anyone in the world of literature today needs to fully comprehend.[10]

This returns CW educators to an ability to discuss racialized identity with the entire class community—for nonwhite and white student-authors alike, this ensures that educators place discussions on the table of what student-authors think to include in their work and how this work engages with potential and target audiences. There's no conversation to have around "the writer's craft" without there also being a discussion of audience and of audience expectation/genre knowledge, but there are also so many ways these expectations/this knowledge gets tied to recognitions of race. Consider, for example, social media calls in 2022 to make the hit TV series *Bridgerton* (set in Regency-era England) more "historically accurate"—which I read as meaning whiter and which I also read as audiences themselves recognizing the very genre conventions around British historical fiction (especially when dealing with royalty) as necessarily centering the lived experiences of white people.

Mura finally notes that

> [w]hether in terms of identity or one's development as a writer or in the task of finishing a book (particularly one's first book), I see writers as constantly embarking on their own mythical journeys. Thus I view the process of writing as a call to change: *We start to write a book in order to become the person who finishes the book.*[11]

Especially for student-authors entering a 400-level course, assignments (in particular the "Identity Notebook") encourage them to consider how their first books might look were they to be written (or at least started) in class. Especially in a nonfiction course that encourages student-authors to think about their first books as either a memoir or a collection of essays, there may be no better avenue than through Mura's "call to change" toward getting student-authors to think about their identities more considerably—also toward the ends of deciding their book's content. In much the same way I can remember being instructed by one professor to "write about childhood because you're now closer to childhood than you'll ever be again" (which I took as direct advice toward ensuring my first book was a memoir or memoir-adjacent), I'll advise student-authors to write about who they know themselves to be, what's closest to their realms of cultural experience, and to combine this with reaching outside themselves toward contrasting where their experiences align (or don't align) with the experiences of others.

A book like Mura's ultimately serves as perfect instructional material for getting intermediate and advanced student-authors to construct their first memoirs/ collections of personal essays. Because the book is so tied, as Mura states, to "an increased focus on the issues of identity" it not just serves to emphasize the CW class community as a space where such nuanced discussion can (and should) take place but also emphasizes how student-authors can track and observe personal growth through the trajectory of their creative writing projects.

# Reflection

When I revisit evaluations from student-authors in introductory courses I see they've written comments about how "[w]e learned about different styles of writing & how to apply them to publication." In terms of the two or three activities/class practices that were most helpful, they've also mentioned "workshops & collaboration." One student-author noted that "[t]he most significant thing I learned was how to write for a specific audience." One question in the evaluation reads: *What was the most significant thing you have learned about writing or about yourself as a writer in this course?* and a student-author wrote, "I learned how to step out of my comfort in academic writing and to explore more in creative writing." Finally, perhaps the most telling evaluative comment I've seen regarding course readings garnered the response of one student-author who wrote that "[t]hey evolved by changing focuses. They invited me to engage with ideas, perspectives, arguments, and genres that I, as a straight white male, wouldn't normally engage with."

What all this together tells me is that a course design focused on a deliberate diversity of readings has allowed student-authors to (1) break away from their "comfort zones" through writing, (2) learn how to consider *audience* beyond just the goals of self-expression, and (3) engage in live dialogue by way of small-group workshops. Comments like these make me continue to think about fusing reading and writing practices in an introductory course, in that student-authors often enter the course not hoping to be assigned a barrage of readings (as this is what they might anticipate from a literature course) but to instead be able to write much and read one another's work often.

If this weren't an introductory course, then at the right level it could be appropriate for there to be few to no assigned readings in the course at all, and have the class focus instead on more peer review. At the introductory level, though, it's especially helpful for student-authors to be able to engage with various styles of nonfiction, read nonfiction from names they might not otherwise see outside of the class, gain practice at pronouncing the names of authors they'd never otherwise have to say out loud, and, finally, view the work of authors from locales they may not be encouraged to consider within the rest of their English/CW curricula.

I'm still insistent at this time about using Adsit's threshold concepts toward bringing student-authors into CW/nonfiction at the Intro level. In future iterations of the course, however, these concepts might also be fused with a themed design like one focused on flash nonfiction.[12]

Part of the challenge of an introductory course (especially at places like my home institution) revolves around attempts to bridge gaps between what happens at the Intro level and what's happening at intermediate and advanced levels. The question is always how to prepare student-authors for what's next, whether it be a 400-level course or an MA/MFA. When it comes solely to the Intro course, though, I've been happy with the ways student-authors and I have been able to engage in group workshop and diverse readings and connect these readings to the more theoretical concerns (i.e., threshold concepts) that help us interrogate what CW is and can do. I've designed the introductory course the way I have for these reasons and am constantly looking forward to how such a course can become even more refined throughout future iterations.

Finally, and by contrast, for the Studies course, feedback included commentary detailing that, for one student-author, the course was about "[d]iscovering ways to navigate reliving difficult experiences through writing in a cathartic way" and this being helpful. Another comment mentioned that the course's second major project, the "Identity Notebook," was "an excellent prompt to tackle an author's identity through writing. With this assignment, I was able to apply a better understanding of my own identity to future memoir writings." What I take from comments like these is that student-authors will capitalize on opportunities (whether in a short or long form) to focus on learning about themselves—and that they're perhaps even more eager to do so if this involves research processes. That is, CW educators might question what it can mean for student-authors to develop senses of responsive critical understanding (à la Graeme Harper) of oneself, rather than just senses of critical understanding around the textual subjects covered in class.

# Conclusions

Curricula centered around Sherry Quan Lee's and/or David Mura's might take issues of cultural dexterity and inclusion to heart, which of course I've tried to focus on implementing in my own courses. Ultimately, I hope other CW educators who, like me, are willing to follow the leads of those like Adsit, Lee, and Mura, might use these leads to continue helping student-authors (and GSIs alike) view the broader dimensions of CW's cultural potential.

In the end, I hope to continue practicing CW pedagogies in an inclusive, transnational, and attentive context. I hope to combine CW pedagogies with conversations already present in areas like sociolinguistics, English Language Teaching, writing studies, and the health humanities—using this combination to offer visibility, accessibility, and a platform not only for those voices of the authors students are unlikely to read in other CW curricula but also for the sake of student-authors who, through seeing themselves reflected in course readings, can come to see that they have a place at the roundtable, too.

# Notes

1  Further enrollment statistics are available at https://institutionalresearch.syr.edu/facts-and-figures/.

2  Also see: Adsit, Janelle. "Reading List." *Critical Creative Writing*, https://www.criticalcreativewriting.org/reading-list.html.

3  Adsit, Janelle. "The Writer and Meta-Knowledge about Writing: Threshold Concepts in Creative Writing." *New Writing: The International Journal for the Practice and Theory of Creative Writing*, vol. 14, no. 3, 2017, pp. 305–15. doi:10.1080/14790726.2017.1299764.

4  Ibid., p. 304.

5  Lee, Sherry Quan. "Introduction." *How Dare We! Write: A Multicultural Creative Writing Discourse*, 2nd ed. Modern History Press, 2022, pp. iii–v. ISBN 978-1-61599-683-4.

6  Ibid., p. iii.

7  Ibid

8  Ibid

9  Mura, David. "Introduction." *A Stranger's Journey: Race, Identity, and Narrative Craft in Writing*. The University of Georgia Press, 2018, pp. 1–7.

10  Ibid., p. 7

11  Ibid.

12  For example, see resources available at *Teaching with The Best of Brevity* (https://brevitymag.com/teaching-best-of-brevity/), which provides potential designs toward providing student-authors a healthy portfolio of brief written work in CW. (Though, this might not prepare them as much to engage in reading and writing longform nonfiction if this is an instructor's goal.)

# Further Reading

Adler, Kassner-Linda and Elizabeth A. Wardle. *Naming What We Know: Threshold Concepts of Writing Studies* (Classroom Edition). Utah State University Press, 2016.

Bauer, Dale M. "Indecent Proposals: Teachers in the Movies." *College English*, vol. 60, no. 3, 1998, pp. 301–17. JSTOR, www.jstor.org/stable/378559.

Brodkey, Linda. "Modernism and the Scene(s) of Writing." *College English*, vol. 49, no. 4, April 1987, pp. 396–418.

Brooke, Robert. "Modeling a Writer's Identity: Reading and Imitation in the Writing Classroom." *College Composition and Communication*, vol. 39, no. 1, 1988, pp. 23–41.

Hoang, Lily and Joshua Marie Wilkinson, editors. *The Force of What's Possible: Writers on Accessibility & the Avant-Garde*. Nightboat Books, 2015.

Malcolm, Janet. *The Journalist and the Murderer*. Vintage Books, 1990.

Meyer, Jan and Ray Land. *Threshold Concepts and Troublesome Knowledge: Linkages to Ways of Thinking and Practising within the Disciplines*. ETL Project, 2003, pp. 1–12.

# 7

# Where We've Been, Where We're Going

## Considerations and Continuations

In the Appendix of Stephanie Vanderslice's *Rethinking Creative Writing in Higher Education: Programs and Practices that Work* (2011), Vanderslice details what they deem an "Honor Roll of Graduate Creative Writing Programs," listing seven graduate programs throughout the continental United States and three in the United Kingdom—featured because these programs "enhance their graduate experience in *at least one* area: teaching, publishing, community service, creative industry connections."[1] Though Vanderslice wasn't able to open the list up to programs outside the United States or the United Kingdom at the time, their work nonetheless serves as an excellent start. It's a beginning that should, at least, get those of us participating in CW programs in North American higher education to consider what might place our programs onto a kind of "honor roll" should organizations like the National Council of Teachers of English (NCTE) or Association of Writers and Writing Programs (AWP) decide to formalize one.

Aside from professionalization options highlighted in Vanderslice's Appendix, I'd also love to see (for CW programs at the undergraduate level) more programs beginning to appear on a kind of honor roll because of their cultural dexterity efforts. Vanderslice notes, for instance, how Wendy Bishop asserts in *Released into Language: Options for Teaching Creative Writing* (1990) that "it is important for students to learn how varied writers' lives are, that there is no one way to pursue a writing career."[2] I want to stress, as we move forward together as CW educators, that it's important to consider these variations in authors' lives and that authors' lives aren't only or always connected to their careers.

For these considerations, these continuations, I begin by thinking about undergraduate programs. CW programs at the undergraduate level, as I've mentioned throughout this book, need a kind of restructuring à la Janelle Adsit, Felicia Rose Chavez, David Mura, Sherry Quan Lee, Matthew Salesses, and more, providing a change in curricula not just around thinking differently about what an "author's life" means but also how such livelihoods make their way into authors' texts. I've written here often that student-authors need to consider the cultural dimensions of others' lives—and in revisiting Vanderslice's honor roll, some additional criteria I'd suggest would be for an expansion of the honor roll based on its ability to incorporate cultural dexterity.

For graduate student instructors (GSIs), it would be encouraging to see CW programs enhance the "teaching" and "community service" components Vanderslice outlines. For the most part I imagine ways GSIs might not just gather pedagogical practice in the undergraduate classrooms of the institutions where they study but also gain practice outside of those classrooms. This is already possible in many programs with outreach in K–12 schools (I completed a K–2 TESOL internship during graduate school, for instance) where experiences teaching creative writing to children can help them further consider how to do so with adults.

GSIs might also supplement (or enact as an alternative) the "critical introduction" components of their theses/dissertations with pedagogical considerations, which could take the issues raised throughout this book even further. For those at the doctoral level, such an alternative can carry a graduate program beyond just the "creative writing and literature" positioning currently enacted by so many programs—an example alternative being found in programs like those at the University of Louisiana Lafayette and its implementing a Creative Writing Studies (CWS) concentration within the PhD.[3]

As beneficial as having more than just an introduction to genres in CW curricula would be for student-authors in undergraduate programs, so would examining how these genres are tied to the cultures from which authors emerge. I hope CW student-authors can become more proficient at discussing issues of (for instance) queer identities, Indigenous identities, immigrant identities, disabled identities, multilingual identities, and so on. This won't happen without remaining open to conversations with student-authors that actually push them toward discussing the contexts tethered to these identities, however.

Only after all this might CW programs not just operate alongside student-authors' twenty-first-century goals, expectations, and standards but also display that CW programs themselves have an ability to stand as a critical part of student-authors' experiences in class communities. Only then—with care, attention, and effort—can CW find itself alongside the areas of study and practice already paving the way forward, and already powered by student-authors' voices, traditions, and senses of self.

# Notes

1 Vanderslice, Stephanie. *Rethinking Creative Writing in Higher Education: Programs and Practices that Work*. Creative Writing Studies, 2011.
2 Bishop, qtd. in ibid., p. 33.
3 A Program of Study for the University of Louisiana Lafayette can be found at https://www.google.com/url?sa=t&rct=j&q=&esrc=s&source=web&cd=2&cad =rja&uact=8&ved=2ahUKEwiwo6jk9OHhAhVKJKwKHTP0DwIQFjABeg QIARAC&url=https%3A%2F%2Fenglish.louisiana.edu%2Fsites%2Fenglish %2Ffiles%2FPlan%2520of%2520Study%2520CW%2520FA17.docx&usg =AOvVaw23HIxY3GuSbt0nkzEfe2eT. (This isn't to note, however, that "CWS concentrations" are necessary for the future of CW programs—they nonetheless signal that graduate programs might remain open to more intensive study as part of a GSI's practice.)

# Appendix A

## Sample Syllabus—Introduction to Creative Nonfiction

### Course Description: Introduction to Creative Nonfiction

In addition to writing-intensive practice in literary/creative nonfiction, this course also involves an introduction to threshold concepts in creative writing (nonfiction) by examining authors' cultural, professional, institutional (including those in academic environments), and theoretical concerns. This course will help beginning student-authors hone their literary practices through reading and composing creative nonfiction through culturally dexterous lenses, specifically through a survey of global nonfiction and/or literary translation.

Considering the elements of brief creative nonfiction (and considering examples covered as a class) discussed throughout the first unit of the course, the first major project asks student-authors to compose a "flash" (700–750 words) nonfiction text. Using course readings as potential models, the flash nonfiction project will allow student-authors to explore reflection and personal experience within a short form.

The second project/unit is designed to allow student-authors to compose either a medium-length (1,500–2,500 words) researched creative nonfiction text based on a writing prompt (listed on the project assignment sheet) *or* a literary translation project (three to five poems) accompanied by a commentary essay.

A third project in the course asks student-authors to survey the landscape of literary publishing, resulting in a 250–300-word publication "write-up" displaying the student-author's familiarity with a chosen literary journal/magazine/anthology/etc. The write-up will also note the publication's history, and how such history intersects with acts of inclusion and/or marginalization.

In a final portfolio/project, student-authors will revise any work they choose (from writing prompts/workshopped writing/major projects) from throughout the course, an additional requirement being that they *target a specific publication of their choice* (the class will be provided a list of options). Considering the threshold concepts and readings from throughout the course, the second part of the portfolio then asks student-authors to respond to two (2) exam questions in the form of short (700–750 words) papers using course readings as illustrations/examples.

## Prerequisite/Corequisite

N/A

## Audience

Students interested in creative nonfiction courses beyond first-year writing/composition.

## Credits

Three credit(s) At least 1x every fall or spring.

## Learning Objectives

After taking this course, student-authors will be able to:

1. Learn to respond to the difficult experiences in classmates' writing with care and through a practice of rhetorical listening.
2. Establish trust in the creative writing class community, both in peer-to-peer relationships and in the instructor/student-author relationship.
3. Prepare to collaborate with peers from diverse language traditions and backgrounds.
4. Interrogate the culturally mediated conventions of genre and craft.
5. Foster cross-cultural knowledge through developing a creative writing research practice and ethic.

# Required Texts/Supplies

- Lee, Sherry Quan, editor. *How Dare We! Write: A Multicultural Creative Writing Discourse*, 2nd ed. Modern History Press, 2022. ISBN 978-1-61599-683-4.
- All other materials will be made available to students on Blackboard or by other digital means.

# Course Requirements and Expectations

*Project #1: Flash Nonfiction.* The first major project asks student-authors to compose a "flash" (700–750 words) nonfiction text. Using course readings as potential models, the flash nonfiction project will allow student-authors to explore reflection and personal experience within a short form. This project targets learning objectives 1, 3, 4, and 5 and includes a reflective component within the project itself.

*Project #2: Researched Nonfiction* or *Literary Translation.* This project is designed to allow student-authors to draft either a medium-length (1,500–2,500 words) researched creative nonfiction project based on a writing prompt (listed on the project assignment sheet) *or* a literary translation project (three to five poems) accompanied by a 1,500–2,500-word commentary essay. Similar to Project #1, this project will include a reflective component and additionally targets objectives 1 through 6.

*Project #3: Publication Write-Up.* To prepare for completion of the final portfolio, the third project in the course asks student-authors to survey the landscape of literary publishing—resulting in a 250–300-word publication "write-up" displaying the student-author's familiarity with a chosen literary journal/magazine/anthology/etc. The write-up will also note the publication's history, and how such history intersects with acts of inclusion and/or marginalization—that is, whom the publication has a history of featuring and not featuring. This project targets objectives 2, 4, and 5.

*Final Portfolio/Project: Submittable Revision + Exam Questions.* For the final portfolio, student-authors will revise any work they choose (from writing prompts/workshopped writing/major projects) from throughout the course, with an additional requirement being that they *target a specific publication of their choice* (the class will be provided a list of options). Student-authors are *not* required to submit their manuscripts; however, they must still *target* their work toward a particular publication—with an accompanying cover letter displaying student-authors' knowledge of the publication's mission/goals/aesthetic.

Then, considering the threshold concepts and readings from throughout the course, the second part of the portfolio asks student-authors to respond to two (2) exam questions in the form of short (700–750 words) papers using course readings as illustrations/examples, to display considerations of creative nonfiction as an area of cultural study and practice.

This project targets objectives 1, 2, 4, and 5.

# Homework and In-Class Activities

In-class activities and homework will include workshopping, writing exercises (in class/on Blackboard), and written peer feedback. These assignments target all learning objectives for the course and scaffold work toward the successful completion of student-authors' Final Portfolios.

# Workshop Groups

During Unit 1, student-authors will begin participating in designated workshop groups, the purpose of which is to provide an opportunity to review (in small groups) the writing from a specific member of the group. In doing so, all group members will be exposed to a variety of student-authored texts, in order to generate ideas as well as receive/provide ideally usable feedback. (Peer feedback worksheets will also be made available.) Workshop groups will consist of four to five students per group, with student-authors taking turns, facilitating the discussion of their own work. (After Unit 1, we can decide together as a class community whether to proceed with the workshop groups, form new groups, or eliminate group workshop altogether.)

# Grade Breakdown

- Project #1 | Flash Nonfiction | 20%
- Project #2 | Researched Nonfiction *or* Literary Translation | 20%
- Project #3 | Publication Write-Up | 10%
- Final Portfolio | Submittable Revision + Exam Questions | 30%
- Ongoing Activities | Summary-Responses/Invention Work/Peer Feedback/ Discussion | 20%

# Appendix B

## Sample Schedule—Introduction to Creative Nonfiction

This schedule is a *working document*, and at any point I may alter a reading or an assignment. If so, you'll always be made aware of any changes to this schedule well in advance (Table 1).

HDWW = *How Dare We! Write*

Table 1 Sample Schedule—Introduction to Creative Nonfiction.

| Week | Topic/Theme/Goal | Reading Due | Writing Due |
|---|---|---|---|
| 1 | Intros & Icebreakers | Adsit, "Unpacking Privilege in Creative Writing"; Huber, "The Three Words That Almost Ruined Me As a Writer" | "Icebreaker: Who I Am" (Bb post) |
| | Assign Projects #1 & #2 | Adsit, "The Writer and Meta-knowledge about Writing"; Monroe, "A Brief History and Theory of the Genre" | |
| 2 | Begin threshold concepts: *Community*; distribute Group Workshop Schedule | "Viet Thanh Nguyen Reveals How Writers' Workshops Can Be Hostile"; Das, "On Parsing" Lopez, "Stories that Must Be Told" (HDWW); Nguyen, "Unsilencing the Writing Workshop" | |
| 3 | Concept: *Authorship* Begin Group Workshops | hooks, "to gloria, who is she" Gay, "Black in Middle America" | Group Workshop #1 |
| 4 | Concept: *Language* | Gonzalez, "Dancing Between Bamboos"; Harmon, "Writing Deaf" | |
| | Workshop | Tang-Bernas, "\'in-glish\'" | Group Workshop #2 |

(*Continued*)

**Table 1** (*Continued*).

| Week | Topic/Theme/Goal | Reading Due | Writing Due |
|---|---|---|---|
| 5 | Concept: *Genre* | Lefferson, "Stories from the Heart of Dark-Eyed Woman" (HDWW) | |
| | Workshop | Boully, "On the EEO Genre Sheet" | Group Workshop #3 |
| 6 | Concept: *Craft* | Gómez R., "It Happened in Fragments" (HDWW) | |
| | **Studio Day/Peer Review** | N/A | **Project #1 due** |
| 7 | **Midterm Conferences** | N/A | N/A |
| | **Midterm Conferences** | N/A | N/A |
| 8 | Concept: *Attention* | Moody et al., "Inappropriate Appropriation" | |
| | Workshop | Hakim Azzam, "How to Erase an Arab" | Group Workshop #4 |
| 9 | Literary Translation | Hedeen, "Dismantling the Myth of Originality" | |
| | | Baudelaire/García Lorca/Zhimo | Translation exercise (in-class) |
| 10 | Concept: *Representation* | Khakpour, "How to Write Iranian America" | |
| | | Boully, "A Short Essay on Being" | Workshop TBD |
| 11 | Concept: *Evaluation*; assign Final Portfolio | Jean So & Wezerek, "Why Is Publishing So White?"; Park Hong, *Minor Feelings* (excerpt pp. 47–57) | |
| | Workshop | Kim, "Fear of an Apocalypse" (HDWW) | Workshop TBD |
| 12 | Concept: *Creativity* | Allery, "mamatowisin" | |
| | **Studio Day/Peer Review** | | **Project #2 Due** |
| 13 | Concept: *Resistance* | Deal-Márquez, "Our Silence Won't Save Us" (HDWW) | |
| | Workshop | Mura, "The Idealized Portrait and the Task of the Writer" | Workshop TBD |
| 14 | Concept: *Revision* | Kaplan, "Anne Frank, Reviser" | |
| | Workshop | Miller, "The Shared Space Between Writer and Reader" | Exam Question sample due (on Bb); workshop TBD |
| 15 | Concept: *Theory* | Achtenberg, "Notes in Journey from a Writer of the Mix" (HDWW) | |
| | **Studio Day/Peer Review** | N/A | N/A |
| Exam | N/A | N/A | N/A |
| Exam | N/A | N/A | **Final Portfolio Due** |

# Appendix C

## Sample Trajectory—Introduction to Creative Nonfiction

### Week 1

During the first class session, the class community will read Janelle Adsit's "Unpacking Privilege in Creative Writing"; an additional in-class reading will include Sonya Huber's "The Three Words That Almost Ruined Me As a Writer: 'Show, Don't Tell.'" On day 1, student-authors will also begin work on a "Who I Am" icebreaker exercise. (Instructions will be distributed in class, with the exercise to later be posted online.)

For the second class meeting, student-authors are to read Adsit's "The Writer and Meta-knowledge about Writing" and Debra Monroe's "A Brief History and Theory of the Genre." Both readings will be foundational to our discussions around creative writing (CW) as an area of study and practice especially for literary/creative nonfiction; Adsit's reading will offer a specific context for the rest of the course.

### Week 2

This week will encompass student-authors beginning to discuss Adsit's "threshold concepts in creative writing," along with course readings that attempt to illustrate how the threshold concepts (1) may play out in nonfiction's context and (2) offer theoretical/practical contexts for further understanding these concepts.

The first concept (rearranged from Adsit's original article) to cover in the course will be *Community*: "Writers are formed by the communities they engage. An analysis of craft must be grounded in an understanding of the varying orientations of readerships. Diverse audiences come to their texts with diverse needs."[1] To help better explain what the *Community* concept can encompass, Adsit also notes that "'Who can access this text?' is a question I regularly pose to my students. They learn to not only question where and how the text circulates, but also to interrogate the assumptions of a text in order to answer this question."[2] Adsit finally notes that being able to conceive of creative writing through *Community* "moves away from the centrality of 'self-expression' and instead emphasises the co-constructed nature of texts, which are developed from a network of relations and intertextuality."[3]

This also serves as an opportunity to use *Community* to discuss the CW workshop as a deep and long-held tradition of CW practices, especially in North American colleges and universities. Although this course isn't strictly a workshop, the class community should still prepare for conversations about how we practice discussing one another's work. That is, how might we better come to understand the expectations around conversations about the writing that takes place *in* our class community? Through such considerations: How might we figure out how best to respond, ourselves, to our peers as community members?

Readings assigned for the week to aid thinking about *Community* in CW include "Viet Thanh Nguyen Reveals How Writer's Workshops Can Be Hostile," Kavita Das's "On Parsing," Luis Lopez's "Stories that Must Be Told" (from *How Dare We! Write*) and Beth Nguyen's "Unsilencing the Writing Workshop." These readings will help us consider how the CW workshop mediates the discussions of those who participate in it—especially when those taking part are marginalized and/or minoritized. Viet Thanh Nguyen, for instance, helpfully reminds us that "[l]iterature and power cannot be separated" and that CW communities' conversations are some of the ways power might become executed/manifest around literary creation & evaluation.[4]

Das's "On Parsing" likewise focuses on Claire Vaye Watkins's "On Pandering" (a suggested but not a required read, to better understand Das's response). Das examines a relationship between CW and feminism, and in doing so helps highlight how white feminism in particular holds patterns of excluding women-identifying nonwhite authors in CW—encouraging us to consider how feminism can operate in CW when such an intersection/relationship becomes more inclusive, rather than exclusive. Lopez's "The Stories that Must Be Told" reflects on Lopez's experiences within the workshop space as a Latine author. Finally, Beth Nguyen's "Unsilencing the Writing Workshop" connects to an intersection between literature and power—on top of the notion that the most "traditional" CW workshop model requires student-authors to remain silent while their peers discuss their work in class (i.e., CW's "gag rule").

# Week 3

This week will focus on the concept of *Authorship*: "Writerly identity is constructed by a range of cultural forces. Cultural messages about the identity and lifestyle of the writer can be critically examined as we gain resources for building a writing life."[5] The class community will consider this concept through bell hooks's "to gloria, who is she: on using a pseudonym" and Roxane Gay's "Black in Middle America." hooks notes how choosing a pseudonym helped lead her to "greater awareness about the relationship between author, identity, and a text."[6] This can help the class community consider what "makes" an author—how an author presents themselves, as well as how authorship gets constructed by the intersection between an author's identity, their composing choices, and any potential target audience(s) for their work. Gay's text, meanwhile, details her experiences as a Black woman living in what are now recognized as Michigan's Upper Peninsula and central Indiana—distinguishing ways that, depending on the geography, Gay's Blackness can be seen as either "more curiosity than threat" or just plain a "threat."[7]

Finally, this week will also begin our group workshops. Student-authors are to observe the workshop schedule (I've scheduled those student-authors who were absent, myself) available in our course documents folder online, and note that group members are currently assigned "#1," "#2," "#3," and so on. Those scheduled for Group Workshop #1 (this week) are to bring in any creative nonfiction draft on which they'd like feedback from peers. Though there's no page length requirement for workshop, please note that *if the text exceeds 10 pp.*, then the text should be distributed prior to class time rather than during, to allow more time for live discussion. Group members are then to provide feedback within forty-eight hours for both the student-author and the instructor to view.

(Finally, student-authors should feel free to negotiate who's "up for workshop" on the schedule among group members. If someone would prefer, for example, to be "#1" rather than "#3," then this will be for the workshop group to decide.)

# Week 4

This week will focus on the concept of *Language*, categorized by Adsit as being that "[l]anguage choices are bound to issues of power. Supporting a polylingual and multimodal literary community requires deliberate attention from writers, which manifests in each writing occasion."[8] Adsit also notes that "[c]reative writers should know language, as the material they work with, for the ways it is tied to identity, culture, history, and power."[9] Readings for the week therefore aim to help the class community consider *Language* as a threshold concept, doing so through Marlina Gonzalez's "Dancing Between Bamboos or The Rules of Wrong Grammar," Kristen Harmon's "Writing Deaf: Textualizing Deaf Literature," and Christina Tang-Bernas's "\'in-glish\."

Beginning with Gonzalez, "Dancing Between Bamboos" can help the class community consider *Language* through Gonzalez having written: "I want to write bilingually. I have always written bilingually. But how does one do that in a culture that insists on erasing my bilinguality, which, by the way, is the result of expeditions and conquests by the very same culture?"[10] Harmon's "Writing Deaf" is meanwhile helpful toward getting us to understand Deafness in a translingual context—Harmon writes, for instance, that the "standards of written English are in many ways incompatible with Deaf meaning-making; this essay explores the implications of this for all creative writers."[11] Finally, Tang-Bernas echoes similar sentiments in a flash nonfiction text focused on how others' language attitudes have impacted their own language practices.

Student-authors scheduled for Group Workshop #2 will also have work due this week.

# Week 5

This week will focus on *Genre* as a threshold concept. Adsit describes this as being that "[t]here are no universal standards for 'good writing': however, there are conventions that are particular to established genres."[12] Adsit also notes how CW "teaches genre conventions and the histories that give rise to the genres we write within" and that considering this threshold concept "gives writers a better sense of what it means to adopt these conventions, what politics might be carried in the continuance of these conventions."[13]

The week's readings intended to help the class community consider this threshold concept further are Olive Lefferson's "Stories from the Heart of Dark-Eyed Woman—Sikadiyaki" and Jenny Boully's "On the EEO Genre Sheet." To begin, Lefferson discusses the process of finding "[her] own place as a writer and a Native in a white world" especially as someone learning to practice creative writing while moving toward the printed page from oral traditions.[14] For Boully, what's potentially helpful is her writing that "[O]ne of my goals as a teacher of nonfiction is to totally destroy every held belief a student has about essays and nonfiction."[15] Boully moves from here into discussing genre categorizations and then parallels them with the categorizations she may be expected to fulfill for others as an author and person of mixed-race heritage and identity.

Group workshop #3 will also take place this week for those student-authors scheduled.

# Week 6

The primary focus for one class session this week will be on wrapping up student-authors' Flash Nonfiction projects. This will include using studio time during class, which additionally serves as an opportunity for peer review.

On top of this week containing the Project #1 due date, student-authors will also explore the *Craft* threshold concept. With a major project being due, the only reading assigned for the week is Isela Xitlali Gómez R.'s "It Happened in Fragments": It may be helpful for student-authors to focus on the writing exercise at the end of Gómez R.'s essay, as the exercise points to ways craft might be considered in the context not just of one's target audience(s) but also in the context of intersecting one's identity with their aims as an author.

# Week 7

This week will involve student-authors' midterm conferences. (Please review the conference schedule I've posted online; I've filled in spaces myself for those absent from class.) Though no work needs to be completed prior to conferences, our conversations will focus on transitioning away from the first unit/project of the course and into the next one. Student-authors should be prepared to discuss their progress in the class and prepare for the work of the second half of the semester.

# Week 8

This week focuses on the *Attention* threshold concept, which is that CW "involves specific modes of attention as writers learn to be close and critical observers of the world. Writers learn to account for the ethical considerations involved in perceiving and reinventing the world through their research and observation."[16] As a class community, we'll use this concept to consider the place of research in CW practices—as Adsit notes, focusing on research in CW can "teach writers the importance of going outside the self and one's received knowledges."[17]

The readings assigned for the week include the panel conversation "Inappropriate Appropriation," Julie Hakim Azzam's "How to Erase an Arab," and "The Soils I Have Eaten" by Aimee Nezhukumatathil. Discussion of Hakim Azzam's and Nezhukumatathil's work will precede Group Workshop #4.

# Week 9

This week will extend student-authors' considerations of the *Language* threshold concept through exploring literary translation as creative writing practice. Assigned readings around these considerations include Katherine M. Hedeen's "Dismantling the Myth of Originality: Translation, Collaboration, Solidarity" and excerpts by Charles Baudelaire, Federico García Lorca, and Xu Zhimo (from Martha Collins's and Kevin Prufer's anthology *Into English: Poems, Translations, Commentaries*). These excerpts allow student-authors to (1) examine how literary translation can act as a CW practice and, perhaps more central to the course, (2) encourage them to examine how the commentary/ translator's essay can be a type of creative nonfiction itself.

To aid student-translators, the week's creative exercise will include making a "trot," or a kind of word-for-word breakdown of a source text in a source language toward a target text/target language. (I'll provide a trot to the class community from Charles Baudelaire's excerpt.) The trot may be especially useful for monolingual student-translators and those interested in practicing translation with a source language they aren't fluent in, familiarizing themselves with literary translation's "beginning blocks." This urges student-authors to overall begin considering how literary translation isn't merely an exercise in creative collaboration but is also, as Katherine Hedeen notes, about remaining "open to otherness."[18]

# Week 10

This week will focus on the threshold concept of *Representation,* noted by Janelle Adsit as being that "[c]reative writing is a form of cultural production. It both reflects and stimulates culture."[19] Adsit also indicates that "[w]riters are shaped by the cultures of which they are part, but they in turn can influence the culture."[20] Readings assigned for the week to illustrate *Representation* include "How to Write Iranian America" by Porochista Khakpour and Jenny Boully's "A Short Essay on Being." The latter focuses on the dish pot Thai as well as on Boully's own national and ethnic identities. Khakpour's text meanwhile examines similar aspects (though unrelated to food) as Boully's but from an editorial perspective, interrogating the assumptions often appearing in communications between herself as an author and the editors with whom she might collaborate as she submits work for publication.

# Week 11

This week focuses on the *Evaluation* threshold concept, described by Janelle Adsit as being that "[l]iterary value is contingent. The evaluation of literature is shaped by cultural and historical forces."[21] To focus not just on "cultural and historical forces" but also on *institutional* forces, there may then be no better way to talk about "literary value" than by discussing publishing practices and the publishing industry.

The class community will begin by engaging with Richard Jean So's and Gus Wezerek's "Just How White Is the Book Industry?" along with an excerpt from Cathy Park Hong's *Minor Feelings: An Asian American Reckoning* (2020) and "Fear of an Apocalypse: Racial Marginalization on the Act of Writing" by Hei

Kyong Kim. Kim notes that "[p]ublication elitism is oppressive and silencing and has caused a huge block to my writing, warped my self-esteem and identity, told me I was not a writer when I am."[22] So and Wezerek meanwhile offer the results of a study providing statistical outcomes in publishing, noting that out of "the 7,124 books for which we identified [an] author's race, 95 percent were written by white people."[23] Finally, Hong writes in "Stand Up," excerpted from *Minor Feelings*, about how literature "supposedly bridges cultural divides, an axiom that rang false once I understood the inequities of the publishing industry"[24] and that "writers of color must tell their stories of racial trauma, but for too long our stories have been shaped by the white imagination. Publishers expect authors to privatize their trauma: an exceptional family or historic tragedy tests the character before they arrive at a revelation of self-affirmation."[25]

The class community will also take time this week to discuss the final portfolio.

# Week 12

This week will be double-barreled in focus in that it examines the *Creativity* threshold concept while also wrapping up the course's second major project. For *Creativity*, student-authors might begin with Adsit's description that "[w]riters benefit from a robust toolkit of applied theoretical frames and process heuristics for generating texts. Principles from creativity studies are useful for increasing the versatility of writers."[26] Adsit also notes how she invites student-authors "to run a number of experiments to see what fosters their own creative thinking. One assignment asks them to remove something that they are used to using, to figure out how to write without it. This might mean writing with their non-dominant hands, writing without a pen or pencil, or writing without the alphabet that they learned in grade school."[27] The class community might carry this a bit further by considering not just the psychology of creativity but what we might also recognize as cultures of creativity.

Nia Allery's "mamatowisin: Writing as Spiritual Praxis" also allows the class community to think through these creative cultures. Allery writes from a Cree perspective, involving that, as a CW educator, she also encourages student-authors to consider creativity from a Cree perspective. Allery writes, referring in part to Michael Hart's "Indigenous Worldviews, Knowledge, and Research Paradigm": "We were going to practice what is described in Cree as *mamatowisin*, 'the capacity to tap the creative life forces of the inner space by the use of all the faculties that constitute our being—it is to exercise inwardness.'"[28]

With Project #2 finally being due this week, for student-authors pursuing the researched nonfiction option it may help them to additionally (though optionally) read "Behind the Writing: On Research," an interview on research and creative writing between Sarah Menkedick, Leslie Jamison, Carina Chocano, and Elena Passarello.[29] For those pursuing the literary translation option, student-authors should remember to focus equally on their commentary essay as a form of nonfiction. (Review Week 9 readings to see how commentary essays might look when they accompany a translation.)

# Week 13

This week focuses on the threshold concept *Revision*, described as being that "[w]riters learn to be responsive to what emerges in the process of creation, as they also bring comparative literary analysis to bear on their revision process."[30] One reading for the week is Deborah E. Kaplan's "Anne Frank, Reviser," which helps student-authors not just examine Frank's *Diary* through a different light and as a text more nuanced than they'd perhaps been led to believe as early readers, but the *Diary* also displays the seriousness with which Frank took her own writing—which she intended to one day meet the public eye. Focusing on Frank's revision practices also helps the class community consider "revision as an explicit topic of discussion, as well as probing beliefs about public and private genres, may also be important when students have little sense of how revising for a general audience can matter to a writer."[31]

In terms of revising literary/creative nonfiction, one reading for the week includes Brenda Miller's "The Shared Space Between Reader and Writer: A Case Study," which introduces student-authors to "hermit crab" texts that "adopt already existing forms as the container for the writing at hand, such as the essay in the form of a 'to-do' list, or a field guide, or a recipe."[32] Miller's essay displays a revision process that eventually leads to "We Regret to Inform You," which takes the form of a rejection letter.

This can help student-authors consider revision as a process while also witnessing how in "allowing form to dictate content," Miller could "bypass what [their] intellectual mind [has] already determined as '[their] story'" and instead "become opened and available to unexpected images, themes and memories."[33] Reading Miller can encourage the class community to consider treating their own revisions like "hermit crabs"—beginning to imagine how their current drafts may come across if the content were to take a completely different form. For example, what if student-authors have written a "traditional" narrative that's then made into a list? What might their flash nonfiction look like rewritten as just one sentence (see examples at https://www.completesentencelit.com/)?

The writing task for the week will be a sample exam question. As a reminder, for student-authors' Final Portfolios they're to answer two exam questions (out of the six posed) so to help them get started, one question should be answered during class/online for early feedback.

# Week 14

This week focuses on *Resistance*, which Janelle Adsit describes as being that "[l] iterature can forward social change and the transformation of culture. Literary production is a unique means of putting the world into question."[34] Adsit also notes that "[c]reative writing is an occasion to consider what it means to engage literature as a form of resistance," and that "the creative writing course can explore the intersections of art and activism."[35] Two readings to connect with this threshold concept include Anaïs Deal-Márquez's "Our Silence Won't Save Us: Recovering the Medicine in Our Stories" and David Mura's "The Idealized Portrait and the Task of the Writer."

# Week 15

The final threshold concept to cover in the course will be *Theory*, described as being that "[h]istorical knowledge of aesthetic theories is important to the practice and craft of writing. Writers write within and against traditions and thus benefit from a robust theoretical knowledgebase of cross-cultural artistic thought."[36] Adsit notes that the CW class community "is a place to examine how far theoretical concepts can take a writer, which forms of text-making these concepts describe or fail to describe. The creative writing classroom can be a place where the things we think we know about writing are re-evaluated and historicised."[37] This leads the class community to Anya Achtenberg's "Notes in Journey from a Writer of the Mix," wherein Achtenberg writes: *"[f]ind your writer's voice,* they say, but my voice is ghost, one or many, including the long back family of ghosts that know me. My voice is occupied, inhabited, speaks to story from shifting, bleeding boundaries."[38]

The class community's last focus will be to assemble student-authors' Final Portfolios. This will involve a final studio/peer review day when student-authors may exchange work for feedback and cover any last points of confusion with the instructor.

# Notes

1  Adsit, Janelle. "The Writer and Meta-Knowledge about Writing: Threshold Concepts in Creative Writing." *New Writing: The International Journal for the Practice and Theory of Creative Writing,* vol. 14, no. 3, 2017, pp. 304–15. doi: 10.1080/14790726.2017.1299764.

2  Ibid., p. 310.

3  Ibid.

4  Nguyen, Viet Thanh. "Viet Thanh Nguyen Reveals How Writers' Workshops Can Be Hostile." *The New York Times,* April 26, 2017, https://www.nytimes.com/2017/04/26/books/review/viet-thanh-nguyen-writers-workshops.html.

5  Adsit, p. 307.

6  hooks, bell. "to gloria, who is she: on using a pseudonym." *Talking Back: Thinking Feminist, Thinking Black.* South End Press, 1989, pp. 160–6.

7  Gay, Roxane. "Black in Middle America." *Brevity: A Journal of Concise Literary Nonfiction,* 12 Sept. 2016, https://brevitymag.com/nonfiction/black-in-middle-america/.

8  Adsit, p. 308.

9  Ibid.

10  Gonzalez, Marlina. "Dancing Between Bamboos or The Rules of Wrong Grammar." *How Dare We! Write: A Multicultural Creative Writing Discourse,* 2nd ed. Modern History Press, 2022, pp. 63–74. ISBN 978-1-61599-683-4.

11  Harmon, Kristen. "Writing Deaf: Textualizing Deaf Literature." *Critical Creative Writing: Essential Readings on the Writer's Craft,* edited by Janelle Adsit, Bloomsbury Academic, an Imprint of Bloomsbury Publishing Plc, 2019, pp. 180–6.

12  Adsit, p. 309.

13  Ibid.

14  Lefferson, Olive. "Stories from the Heart of Dark-Eyed Woman—Sikadiyaki." *How Dare We! Write: A Multicultural Creative Writing Discourse,* 2nd ed. Modern History Press, 2022, pp. 167–72. ISBN 978-1-61599-683-4.

15  Boully, Jenny. *Betwixt-and-Between: Essays on the Writing Life.* Coffee House Press, 2018.

16  Adsit, p. 305.

17  Ibid., p. 306.

18  Hedeen, Katherine M. "Dismantling the Myth of Originality: Translation, Collaboration, Solidarity." *Action Books,* April 30, 2020, https://actionbooks .org/2020/04/dismantling-the-myth-of-originality-translation-collaboration -solidarity-by-katherine-m-hedeen/.

19  Adsit, p. 311.

20  Ibid., p. 312.

21  Ibid., p. 311.

22  Kim, Hei Kyong. "Fear of an Apocalypse." *How Dare We! Write: A Multicultural Creative Writing Discourse,* 2nd ed. Modern History Press, 2022, pp. 140–5. ISBN 978-1-61599-683-4.

23  So, Richard Jean, and Gus Wezerek. "Just How White Is the Book Industry?" *The New York Times,* December 11, 2020, https://www.nytimes.com/interactive/2020 /12/11/opinion/culture/diversity-publishing-industry.html.

24  Hong, Cathy Park. *Minor Feelings: An Asian American Reckoning.* One World, an Imprint of Random House, 2020.

25  Ibid., p. 49.

26  Adsit, p. 306.

27  Ibid.

28  Allery, Nia. "mamatowisin: Writing as Spiritual Practice." *How Dare We! Write: A Multicultural Creative Writing Discourse,* 2nd ed. Modern History Press, 2022, pp. 36–42. ISBN 978-1-61599-683-4.

29  Interview available at https://longreads.com/2019/02/07/behind-the-writing-on -research/#more-120191.

30   Adsit, p. 313.

31   Kaplan, Deborah E. "Anne Frank, Reviser." *Pedagogy: Critical Approaches to Teaching Literature, Language, Composition, and Culture*, vol. 18, no. 1, January 2018, pp. 87–107.

32   Miller, Brenda. "The Shared Space Between Reader and Writer: A Case Study." *Brevity: A Journal of Concise Literary Nonfiction*, January 7, 2015, https://brevitymag.com/craft-essays/the-shared-space/.

33   Ibid.

34   Adsit, p. 312.

35   Ibid.

36   Ibid., p. 313.

37   Ibid.

38   Achtenberg, Anya. "Notes in Journey from a Writer of the Mix." *How Dare We! Write: A Multicultural Creative Writing Discourse*, 2nd ed. Modern History Press, 2022, pp. 98–108. ISBN 978-1-61599-683-4.

# Further Reading

Adichie, Chimamanda Ngozi. "The Danger of a Single Story." *TED Talk*, July 2009, https://www.ted.com/talks/chimamanda_ngozi_adichie_the_danger_of_a_single_story?language=en.

Collins, Martha and Kevin Prufer, editors. *Into English: Poems, Translations, Commentaries*. Graywolf Press, 2017.

Hart, Michael. "Indigenous Worldviews, Knowledge, and Research: The Development of an Indigenous Research Paradigm." *Journal of Indigenous Voices in Social Work*, vol. 1, no. 1, February 2010, pp. 1–16.

Menkedick, Sarah. "Behind the Writing: On Research." *Longreads*, February 2019, https://longreads.com/2019/02/07/behind-the-writing-on-research/#more-120191.

Watkins, Claire Vaye. "On Pandering." *Tin House*, 2015, https://tinhouse.com/on-pandering.

# Appendix D

## Sample Syllabus—Studies in Creative Nonfiction

### Course Description: Studies in Creative Nonfiction

How might we utilize literary/creative nonfiction as a tool to explore our and others' social identities? How can studying and practicing creative nonfiction forms help address the conditions affecting people from minoritized and/ or marginalized identities? To explore these questions and more, this course surveys a selection of texts pointed toward the numerous cultural exigencies surrounding creative nonfiction. The authors surveyed in the class will focus on lived experiences of racism, sexism, ableism, and so on—particularly toward utilizing memoir and the essay to investigate the intersection between identity, power, and social bias(es).

The first unit will result in a "flash" (700–750 words) nonfiction (essay or memoir) text asking student-authors to focus on detailing the first realizations of an aspect of their identity. This could include but not be limited to their racialized identities, gendered identities, disabled/nondisabled identities, sexual orientations, income levels, regional/geographical identities, generational identities, and so on.

The second unit will focus on student-authors composing an "Identity Notebook." In a medium-length (1,500–2,500 words) text, student-authors will address questions from David Mura's *A Stranger's Journey* to explore their identities through history—particularly family history in contrast to their own lived experiences.

In the last unit, student-authors will revise any work they choose (from writing prompts/workshopped writing/major projects) from throughout the course into a final portfolio, along with a reflection detailing how texts produced and/or consumed throughout the course have affected their considerations of the relationship between identity and creative nonfiction.

# Prerequisite/Corequisite

Introduction to Creative Nonfiction.

# Audience

Students interested in creative writing courses beyond introductory creative nonfiction.

# Credits

Three credit(s) At least 1x every fall or spring.

# Learning Objectives

After taking this course, students will be able to:

1. Read and critically engage with literary/creative nonfiction texts representing a diverse range of topics, subgenres, and perspectives.
2. Learn about, and critically consider, conventions and characteristics of creative nonfiction throughout its diverse traditions.
3. Explore relationships between creative nonfiction and research, to practice incorporating research into student-authored texts.
4. Develop an awareness of diverse and public audiences, working to construct an authorship responding to audiences' expectations.
5. Experiment with various styles and forms of creative nonfiction.
6. Reflect on their (creative) composing practices and processes.

# Required Texts/Supplies

- Mura, David. *A Stranger's Journey: Race, Identity, and Narrative Craft in Writing.* University of Georgia Press, 2018. ISBN 978-0-82035-346-3
- All other materials will be made available to students on Blackboard or other digital means.

# Course Requirements and Expectations

*Project #1: Flash Nonfiction.* The first major project of the course is a piece of "flash" (700–750 words) nonfiction (essay/memoir) asking student-authors to compose a text focused on a narrative detailing the first realizations of an aspect of their identity. This could include but not be limited to their racialized identities, gendered identities, disabled/nondisabled identities, sexual orientations, income levels, regional/geographic identities, generational identities, and so on. This project targets outcomes 1, 2, 4, and 5 and includes a reflective component within the project itself.

*Project #2: Identity Notebook.* Within a medium-length (1,500–2,500 words) memoir or essay form, student-authors will address the following questions from Mura's *A Stranger's Journey*: *Who am I? Who are my people? What history led to and produced me? What is the history I never learned that I need to know in order to know who I am? What is my buried history? What is the buried history of my people? My family? My country?* Using this prompt, the second major project of the course guides student-authors toward exploring their identities through history—particularly family history in contrast to their own lived experiences. This project targets outcomes 1 through 4.

*Final Portfolio: Revision + Reflection.* For the Final Portfolio, student-authors will revise any previous work chosen from throughout the course (prompted writing/workshopped writing/major projects) into a standalone nonfiction excerpt—along with a reflection detailing how texts produced and/or consumed throughout the course have affected their considerations of the relationship between identity and creative nonfiction. The project targets outcomes 1, 2, 3, and 6.

# Homework and In-Class Activities

In-class activities and homework will include workshopping, writing exercises (in-class/on Blackboard), and written peer feedback. These assignments target all learning objectives for the course and scaffold work toward successful completion of student-authors' Final Portfolios.

# Workshop Groups

During Unit 1, student-authors will begin participating in designated Workshop Groups, the purpose of which is to provide an opportunity to review, in small groups, the creative writing of a specific member of the group. In doing so, all group members will be exposed to a variety of student-authored texts, in order to generate ideas as well as receive/provide ideally usable feedback. (Peer feedback worksheets will also be made available.) Workshop groups will consist of four to five students per group, with student-authors taking turns, facilitating the discussion of their own work. (After Unit 1, we can decide together as a class community whether to proceed with the workshop groups, form new groups, or eliminate group workshop altogether.)

# Grade Breakdown

- Project #1 | Flash Nonfiction | 30%
- Project #2 | Identity Notebook | 30%
- Final Portfolio | Revision + Reflection + 30%
- Ongoing Activities | Prompt Writing/Peer Feedback/Workshopping | 10%

# Appendix E

## Sample Schedule—Studies in Creative Nonfiction

This schedule is *a working document*, and at any point I may alter a reading or an assignment. If so, you'll always be made aware of any changes to this schedule well in advance (Table 2).

**Table 2** Sample Schedule—Studies in Creative Nonfiction.

| Week | Topic/Theme/Goal | Reading (Due Before Class) | Writing (Due by End of Day) |
|---|---|---|---|
| 1 | Intros & Icebreakers | Course Syllabus | |
| | Assign Flash Nonfiction; distribute Workshop Schedule | Bourelle, "Creative Nonfiction in the Composition Classroom"; Geller, "Blood; Quantum" | Bb post: "Who I Am" |
| 2 | | Mura, "Introduction" & "The Search for Identity"; Jackson-Taffa, "My Cousin's Backyard" | Mura, "Some Questions about Process" |
| | Begin Group Workshops | Mura, "The Idealized Portrait and the Task of the Writer"; Osman, "Fluency" | Group Workshop #1 |
| 3 | | Mura, "On Race and Craft"; Baldwin, "The Price of the Ticket" | |
| | Workshop | Flash NF TBD | Group Workshop #2 |
| 4 | | Mura, "The Four Questions of the Narrator in Memoir"; flash NF TBD | |
| | Workshop | Flash NF TBD | Group Workshop #3 |

*(Continued)*

**Table 2** (*Continued*).

| Week | Topic/Theme/Goal | Reading (Due Before Class) | Writing (Due by End of Day) |
|------|------------------|----------------------------|------------------------------|
| 5 | Assign Identity Notebook | Mura, "The Past and the Present Self in Memoir"; Kingston, "No Name Woman" | |
| | Workshop | Flash NF TBD | Group Workshop #4 |
| 6 | | Mura, "Story and Narrative Structure in Memoir"; flash NF TBD | |
| | Studio Day/Peer Review | N/A | **Project #1 Due** |
| 7 | **Midterm Conferences** | N/A | N/A |
| | **Midterm Conferences** | N/A | N/A |
| 8 | **Spring Break** | N/A | N/A |
| | **Spring Break** | N/A | N/A |
| 9 | Memoir & The Essay | Hampl, "Memory & Imagination"; Mura, "The Use of the Reflective Voice in Memoir" | |
| | Workshop | TBD | Group Workshop #5 |
| 10 | Peer Review | N/A | N/A |
| | Studio Day | N/A | **Project #2 Due** |
| 11 | Assign Final Portfolio | Mura, "The Reliability of the Narrator in Memoir"; TBD | |
| | Workshop | TBD | Group Workshop #6 |
| 12 | | Mura, "Narrative Drama in *Cherry* and *Volcano*"; TBD | |
| | Workshop | TBD | Group Workshop #7 |
| 13 | | Mura, "The Writer and the Hero's Journey" | |
| | Cover letters; workshop | TBD | Group Workshop #8 |
| 14 | **Final Project Conferences** | N/A | N/A |
| | **Final Project Conferences** | N/A | N/A |
| 15 | Workshop | | Final Workshop |
| | Studio Day/Peer Review | | |
| Exam | | | |
| Exam | | | **Final Portfolio Due** |

# Appendix F

## Sample Trajectory—Studies in Creative Nonfiction

### Week 1

In addition to class community introductions and icebreakers, the first week of the course will introduce student-authors to discussions around the potential social dimensions of literary/creative nonfiction. This will involve the first assigned reading being Andrew Bourelle's "Creative Nonfiction in the Composition Classroom: Rethinking Antithetical Pedagogies." Additionally, student-authors will start exploring flash nonfiction possibilities, starting with Danielle Geller's "Blood; Quantum" (to be read and discussed in class) as a first sample text.

### Week 2

The second week will guide the class community further into our flash nonfiction unit, as well as begin work with David Mura's *A Stranger's Journey: Race, Identity, and Narrative Craft in Writing*. To start these considerations, assigned readings for the week include Mura's Introduction and "The Search for Identity: A Stranger's Journey," as well as Deborah Jackson-Taffa's "My Cousin's Backyard." For this week, student-authors are also to read Mura's "The Idealized Portrait and the Task of the Writer." For this week's writing, student-authors will address Mura's assignment "Some Questions about Process" (to be submitted by the end of the week).

This week will also begin our group workshops. (Please observe the workshop schedule within our course document packet.) Those scheduled for group workshop #1 will bring in any creative nonfiction on which they'd like to receive peer feedback—I'll provide more specific instructions for submitting work/feedback during class, so those scheduled to bring work in for the first workshop session only need to ensure that they have the means (digital or printed) to distribute the work itself. A final note: If those scheduled for the first session intend to workshop a text 10pp. or more in length, then it should be distributed to the rest of the workshop group prior to class, rather than during.

# Week 3

The class will continue group workshops this week, focusing on those student-authors scheduled as #2. Please remain attentive to workshop groups as outlined online, as this is where any work (CNF and peer feedback) must be submitted for grading. Original creative work and feedback should also be submitted online *within 24 hours*, with the deadline posted as being the day after workshop.

Prior to workshop, readings for the week will entail Mura's chapter "On Race and Craft: Tradition and the Individual Talent Revised" as well as James Baldwin's essay "The Price of the Ticket." Discussion will focus on these two texts, and how they can help influence student-authors' understandings of potential relationships between identity/ies and creative nonfiction.

# Week 4

As the class community heads into Week 4, student-authors will begin exploring questions around narrative and identity in memoir. This will begin with Mura's "The Four Questions of the Narrator in Memoir: Marguerite Duras's *The Lover* and Mary Karr's *The Liars' Club.*" As Mura writes, these four questions are: "Who is the narrator? To whom is the narrator telling the story? When is a narrator telling the story? Why is the narrator telling the story?"[1] This exploration will be accompanied by a flash piece covered in class, as well as a writing activity.

The week will also focus on group workshop #3; in addition to workshop, we'll cover another flash text during class time.

# Week 5

For this week, student-authors are to have read Mura's "The Past and Present Self in Memoir, Vivian Gornick's *Fierce Attachments*, Maxine Hong Kingston's *The Woman Warrior*," and Hong Kingston's "No Name Woman." Following group workshop #4, we'll discuss these two readings as a class community, along with potential options for moving on from the class's first round of workshops.

# Week 6

This week will focus on student-authors' completion of Project #1: Flash Nonfiction. As such, in addition to an in-class reading, student-authors are to read Mura's "Story and Narrative Structure in Memoir," in which Mura focuses on how "it is only as an adult that the author possesses the resources, maturity, strength, and freedom to access the truth of the past and survive."[22] In class, we'll discuss this chapter on top of taking some time to review parameters for Project #2: The Identity Notebook.

One class this week will be run as a Studio Day. This will entail in-class work/peer review on Project #1—student-authors should bring any work into class that serves as progress toward project completion as well as prepare for discussions with peers/myself about any progress made thus far.

# Week 7

This week will concentrate on student-authors' Midterm Conferences. (Student-authors should review the conference schedule online—I've filled in spaces myself for anyone who was absent from class.) Though no work is required prior to conferences, these conversations will focus on transitioning away from the first unit/project of the course and into the next one. Student-authors should be prepared to discuss their own progress in the class and prepare for the work of the second half of the semester.

# Week 8

This week will focus first on distinguishing memoir from the essay as creative nonfiction subgenres. To begin these distinctions, readings assigned include Patricia Hampl's "Memory and Imagination" and Mura's "The Use of the Reflective Voice in Memoir." In addition to covering these readings, as discussed during midterm conferences the class community will also partake in randomized (i.e., not group-assigned) workshops during one class session per week.

We'll then resume group workshops during the other class day, with discussions focused on student-authors assigned for group workshop #5. (In-class reading TBD.) Aside from workshop feedback, there is no writing due.

# Week 9

This week will focus on wrapping up Project #2. As such, the class community will focus on peer review—though student-authors' drafts do not need to be finished by this time, there should be enough of the project completed to be shared with a peer in class. Class time will again serve as studio time, where in-class work (and additional peer review, if desired) will take place to prepare for project submission.

# Week 10

This week will begin by emphasizing the parameters for the Final Portfolio, which will be introduced and discussed during class. Student-authors will also participate in randomized workshop one day this week, and the assigned reading for discussion will be Mura's chapter "The Reliability of the Narrator in Memoir."

The class community will also focus on group workshop #6, with discussion focused on student-authors scheduled to workshop that day.

# Week 11

Although there's no overarching theme for the week, the class will continue our process of workshopping during both class sessions. Followed by in-class writing, discussion will focus in part on Mura's chapter "Narrative Drama in Mary Karr's *Cherry* and Garrett Hongo's *Volcano.*" One class this week will then focus on group workshop #7, with discussion focused on the work of student-authors scheduled to workshop.

## Week 12

This week will involve the class community wrapping up our work with David Mura, concluding with Mura's chapter "The Writer and the Hero's Journey." Any in-class writing will also pertain to this chapter and serve as connective tissue to student-authors' reflections for the Final Project.

The class community will also participate in group workshop #8, which will serve as the final workshop session of the semester. Additionally, one day this week will serve as an opportunity for student-authors to begin reviewing final revisions, prior to completion of the portfolio for the course.

## Week 13

This week will focus on final project conferences. (Student-authors should review the schedule posted online to note their conference day/time.) Conference discussions will focus on concretizing student-authors' ideas for their Final Portfolios; student-authors should be prepared to discuss any progress made toward preparing for the last peer review session of the semester, as well as answer a series of questions about the portfolio from the instructor.

## Week 14

During the week of Final Exams, I'll maintain open/extended office hours (on Zoom) beyond those listed on the syllabus. Student-authors may email me to make an appointment, should they need one.

At the beginning of the week, I'll open a submission window on Blackboard for student-authors to submit Final Portfolios. The Portfolio deadline is Thursday by 11:59 p.m.

Instructions for submitting the Final: Submit just one file, in either Word or Google Doc format. The first page should be a cover letter, addressed to the student-author's targeted publication. This should be immediately followed by their CNF revision, and the document should end with the student-author's reflection.

Any revised work from earlier in the semester that student-authors wish to submit must also be in by the deadline to be reviewed. (*Only* revisions will be reviewed at this time; new work will not be accepted.)

Finally, an Author's Note is *not* required. If student-authors include an Author's Note with their Final Portfolios, then I'll provide both feedback and a grade. If no Author's Note is included, then I will only provide a grade.

# Notes

1  Mura, David. *A Stranger's Journey: Race, Identity, and Narrative Craft in Writing.* The University of Georgia Press, 2018.

2  Ibid., p. 164.

# Appendix G

## Sample Project—Flash Nonfiction

### Description

Refer to p. 244 of David Mura's *A Stranger's Journey*. Mura instructs: "Write about the first time you became aware of or discovered your racial identity. [. . .] Do this assignment with other facets of your identity that are particularly relevant to your writing: gender, orientation, class, region, generation, and so on."[1]

In this project, you'll compose a piece of "flash" (700–750 words) nonfiction (essay/memoir) which focuses on a narrative detailing the first realizations of an aspect of your identity. This could include, but not be limited to: your racialized identities, gendered identities, disabled/ nondisabled identities, sexual orientations, income levels, regional/ geographic identities, generational identities, and so on. Using Janelle Hanchett's essay "How I Discovered I am White" (emailed to student-authors) as a potential example, you might draft your own text using a working title like "How I Discovered I am [. . .]." Beginning with a title like this one, which kind of narrative do you imagine?

Use course readings as examples of flash texts toward the kinds of forms/ subjects your own might cover. Finally, when submitting your draft to the instructor, include an Author's Note (approximately three paragraphs preceding the essay; a sample will be provided) describing your creation and revision processes/techniques, as well as the kind of feedback you're seeking for your draft.

# Criteria Overview

- Project includes an Author's Note of approximately three paragraphs, which details writing and revision strategies, and feedback sought from the instructor.
- Project meets required length (700–750 words).
- Project uses a writing style and voice appropriate for a diverse and public audience.
- Project communicates a sense of personal experience and/or reflection within a short form.
- Project is submitted on time.
- Project follows standard MLA 9 conventions of formatting, proofreading, and citation (where necessary) containing few or no surface-level issues.

# Note

1   Mura, David. *A Stranger's Journey: Race, Identity, and Narrative Craft in Writing.* The University of Georgia Press, 2018.

# Appendix H

## Sample Project—Researched Nonfiction *or* Literary Translation

### Description

This project in the course is designed to allow you to compose *either* a piece of medium-length (1,500–2,500 words) researched literary nonfiction, based on a writing prompt (listed below), *or* a literary translation project (three to five poems, accompanied by a 1,200–3,600-word commentary essay).

### Option #1: Researched Literary Nonfiction

**Prompts below:**

- Draft a literary/creative nonfiction text utilizing research on immigration in the United States.
- Draft a text that is helpful to the #AllBlackLivesMatter movement.
- Draft a text that is helpful to survivors of sexual violence.
- Draft a text that utilizes research on an environmental or public health crisis within the last five years.
- Draft a text exploring a dialect or language policy in a particular environment (e.g., in public schools).
- Draft a text focused on an issue within a specific geography outside the United States.

# Option #2: Literary Translation (plus commentary essay)

To explore a relationship between literary translation and nonfiction, you might also complete a translation project in combination with a commentary essay (on your translation itself). In this project you must keep in mind the ways content, form, and notions of anticolonial translation come together in your translation. (Use course readings for reference.) Begin by searching for three to five poems you've chosen to translate, and then accompany your translations with an articulation of your translation choices in a 1,200–3,600-word commentary essay.

# Instructions for Option #1

Begin by selecting a news article (don't use a feature story, however) related to your chosen prompt from the prompt list given. Compose your draft by first summarizing any narrative details in your own words. That is, make your source text more elaborate/vivid through your own rhetorical choices and considerations. Finally, consider: What is it about this event/situation that stands out to you as the researcher? What's your reason for choosing this topic?

# Instructions for Option #2

Similar to the trot exercise introduced in class, begin by creating your own trot from your selected author's source text. Your first draft should encompass both the trot and your translation together—eventually working toward a fuller collection (of three to five poems) along with your commentary essay.

# Criteria Overview

- *For all projects:* Includes a prefatory Author's Note of approximately three paragraphs, which details writing and revision strategies, and feedback sought from the instructor.

- *For all projects:* Writing style/tone is appropriate for a diverse and public (nonacademic) audience.
- *For all projects:* Follows standard MLA 9 conventions of formatting, proofreading, and citation (where necessary) containing few or no surface-level issues. (Poetry may be single spaced.)
- *For all projects:* Meets required length: 1,500–2,500 words for researched nonfiction or three to five poems accompanied by a 1,200–3,600-word commentary essay.
- *For Researched Nonfiction:* Successfully follows a writing prompt selected from the list on the project assignment sheet.
- *For Literary Translation:* Poems are compiled in successive pages, with the source text/language appearing, for example, on p. 1 and the translation appearing on p. 2.
- *For Literary Translation:* Translations are accompanied by a commentary essay (1,200–3,600 words) introducing the source author, explaining your process as a translator, and positioning the author within their geography and time period. You may also explore why you chose to translate this particular author, what your own connection to them might be, and any potential issues with bringing their text into English. Your goal is to compose a thoughtful essay that will open the door for Anglophone readers to appreciate the work of the author you've chosen.

# Appendix I

## Sample Project—Identity Notebook

### Description

Refer to p. 243 of David Mura's *A Stranger's Journey*. Mura writes: "Keep a notebook. A book about claiming your identity. A notebook asking, 'Who am I?' [. . .] The subject of this notebook is 'you.' Your identity. Your racial and ethnic identity. And any other ways you choose to identify yourself—gender, sexuality, class, region, country, family, immigrant, and so on."[1]

Particular questions (from Mura) to pursue in this project are as follows: *Who am I? Who are my people? What history led to and produced me? What is the history I never learned that I need to know in order to know who I am? What is my buried history? What is the buried history of my people? My family? My country?*

Beginning with these specific questions, in this project you'll draft a medium-length (1,500–2,500 words) text in a memoir or essay form. The project overall allows you to explore your identity through history—particularly family history in contrast to your own lived experiences.

### Criteria Overview

- Project includes a prefatory Author's Note of approximately three paragraphs, which details writing and revision strategies, and feedback sought from the instructor.
- Addresses questions present within the assignment prompt.
- Explores identity through a connection between history, family history, and lived experience.

- Uses a writing style and voice appropriate for a diverse and public audience.
- Meets required length (1,500–2,500 words).
- Is submitted on time.
- Follows standard MLA 9 conventions of formatting, proofreading, and citation (where necessary), containing few or no surface-level issues.

# Note

1  Mura, David. *A Stranger's Journey: Race, Identity, and Narrative Craft in Writing.* The University of Georgia Press, 2018.

# Appendix J

## Sample Project—Revision for Targeted Publication + Exam Questions

### Part 1: Revision for Targeted Publication

In the first part of your Final Portfolio, you'll revise any work you choose from throughout the course (e.g., prompt writing, workshopped writing, or major projects) with an additional requirement being that you *target a specific publication of your choice*. Options may be found in the list provided in Table 3.

**Publication List**

Though not exhaustive, your publication may be chosen from the following list (links are included to publication websites/submission guidelines):

(The table has been generated from a *Newpages* "Call for Submissions" list detailing publications seeking submissions as of April 2022.)

**Table 3** Publication List.

| | |
|---|---|
| *Brevity: A Journal of Concise Literary Nonfiction* | *Oyster River Pages* |
| | *Palooka* |
| *Complete Sentence: A Magazine of Single-Sentence Prose* | *Parhelion Literary Magazine* |
| | *Pensive: A Global Journey of Spirituality & the Arts* |
| *Hippocampus Magazine: Memorable Creative Nonfiction* | |
| | *Plant-Human Quarterly* |
| *LIGHT (Leaders Igniting Generational Healing & Transformation)* | *They Call Us* |

# Part 2: Responses to Exam Questions

Considering CW threshold concepts and readings discussed throughout the course, the second part of the portfolio asks you to respond to two (2) exam questions in the form of short (750–1,000 words) papers using course readings as illustrations/examples/evidence. One exam essay will be completed in class, while the other will be submitted along with your Final. Again, you must choose two out of the following six questions:

1. What is *authorship*?
2. How can literary/creative nonfiction be practiced/researched/examined for its translingual potential?
3. If authors are formed by the traditions and communities from which they come, how might they compose creative nonfiction for diverse readerships?
4. How might creative nonfiction authors avoid issues of misrepresentation (or misappropriation) in their writing?
5. How might new media and twenty-first-century technologies affect the ways we compose and consume creative nonfiction?
6. In which ways might creative nonfiction writing operate specifically as a method of political action?

## Criteria Overview

- *(For CNF revision)*: Includes a professionalized cover letter addressed to (the editors of) the student-author's target publication.
- *(For CNF revision)*: Is an engaging, imaginative, and thoughtful piece of literary/creative nonfiction that successfully demonstrates an understanding of the publication's objectives/values/aesthetic.
- *(For CNF revision)*: Meets selected publication's required length.
- *(For Exam Responses)*: Provides effective critical thought and synthesis of course content (e.g., threshold concepts and readings) through careful responses to exam questions.
- *(For Exam Responses)*: Use of a writing style and tone appropriate for an academic audience.

- *(For Exam Responses):* Follows standard MLA 9 conventions of proofreading and citation (where necessary), containing few or no surface-level issues.
- Project is submitted on time.

# Index

CPSIA information can be obtained
at www.ICGtesting.com
Printed in the USA
LVHW070410080623
749234LV00004B/18